Kitten Kindergarten

SABINE SCHROLL

Kitten Kindergarten

How to educate your kitten successfully
from the very first day

Bibliographical Information of the Deutsche Nationalbibliothek
This publication is listed in the Deutsche Nationalbibliographie
of the Deutsche Nationalbibliothek;
detailed bibliographical information can be accessed
under http: //dnb.d-nb.de

© 2017 Sabine Schroll
Printing, Production and Layout:
BoD – Books on Demand

ISBN 978-3-7431-1118-9

Table of contents

Foreword 9
   ... and they can be trained! 10

What does education really mean? 11
   Educating means pulling, not pushing! 12
   Why should cats be educated? 13
   It's a matter of creating a relationship 16
   Educating cats is a challenge 16
   Educating cats –
   won't it be terribly time-consuming? 19

The raw materials 23
   The first learning process – socialisation 26
   How do I choose a kitten? 29
   Is there an ideal time for adopting a kitten? 36
   When do you start educating a cat? 37

What is a well educated cat? 39
   All a question of motivation 40
      ..., because it's a cat 40
      ..., because it's fun! 41
      ..., because it's hungry 42
      ..., because it needs something 43
      ..., because it's curious 43
      ..., because it is ill 44
      ..., because it's frightened 44

**The feline household –
creating an environment to be good in** 47
   Feeding 48
   Water supply 56
   Litter box 59

Scratch marking facilities 62
  Climbing facilities – the third dimension 64
  Resting and hiding places 67
  The transport box 70
  Entertainment 73
  Safety 88
  Access to the outdoors 94
  Basic kit – what do cats need? 102

Development 103

The first step – learning to learn 105
  How cats learn – the theory 105
  How cats learn – in practice 110
    Formal and informal clicking 111
    Classical conditioning in training 112
    What constitutes a reward for cats? 112

The first three exercises. 117
  Nose target 117
  Paw target 119
  Sitting target 121

Other important exercises for everyday 125
  Its own name 125
  Coming when called or whistled for 126
  Lifting up 127
  Sitting 129
  Eye contact 130
  Confined sitting 131
  Sitting in a specific place 133
  Lying on the side 135
  Lying on the back 136
  Tolerance for handling and personal care 138
  Giving tablets 144
  Bathing 151

  Learning words 153
  Harness and leash 156
  Thundershirt® 159
  Transport box 162
  Controlled play 166
  Tricks 167
 Having experiences 168

Competence in solving problems 177

What about things that aren't allowed? 187
  Mine! 190
  Leave it! 191
  Negative conditioning 193
 When it doesn't seem to be working 197

Kitten kindergarten 201

Educating several cats 203

And how about older cats? 207

Side-effects of education 209

Life skills 211

Training plan 213
  Exercises to be practised several times a day 214
  Daily exercises 215
  Exercises for practising once or twice a week 215
  One-off exercises 216

Afterword 217
Resources 219
Index 221

Foreword

While I was working on this book, my blue Abyssinian cat *Skyboy* fell ill with a malignant lymphoma at the age of eight months. Within just a few weeks, as a young cat, he had already acquired an extremely wide repertoire of terms and words, actions, exercises and tolerance of manipulation. And I could never have dreamed that all these life skills such as only a cat can have would be so soon and so harshly put to the test in the real world of diagnosis and therapy.

Skyboy is – along with all the other cats I have known and loved, and that have influenced me over the years – the cat who affected me most and touched me most deeply. He was the first cat in my kitten kindergarten, and was trained in accordance with this plan. In our ten months together, he changed my point of view and my way of relating to cats more than all the others before him.

Skyboy survived his first birthday by one month – but his legacy lives on…

Be inspired by *Skyboy's* star dust, and play with him by giving your cat a touch of him!

Skyboy

... and they can be trained!

For most dog owners these days it is automatic to take their puppy to a puppy school and play group for young dogs, and later on attend a training course. No doubt about it, dogs need to be educated. But cats? ... You can hardly expect them to cooperate!

But is this really true? Why shouldn't cats – who are so exceedingly quick and eager to learn, especially when they expect to be rewarded – actually acquire important skills for living with us, with the help of proactive and systematically devised education? What would it be like if we were to offer cats too a planned and structured course of education, so as to make our life together more beautiful and harmonious?

What does education really mean?

One of the reasons why cats are generally seen as ineducable is a picture that comes from dog training, and sad to say is still frequently met with in that context: a tight collar, a sharp tug on the leash and all manner of drilling and discipline are applied so that eventually a *well educated* dog emerges, one who immediately obeys all commands without any ifs or buts. But even if, thank goodness, dog training is no longer viewed in such a harsh military light, the idea of using a systematic strategy to train a cat is still strange and unfamiliar, so that educating a cat is likely to be seen, right from the start, as senseless and utterly impossible. A cat should be left to develop freely and independently, and allowed on the whole to do what it wants to do – unless we find its behaviour upsetting. But all this bears only a very peripheral relation – if it has one at all – to educating in the true sense of the word!

Perhaps it doesn't actually have to do with cats, but rather with the way in which training is seen, generally speaking, and the way it is carried out – could that be the reason why cats are still thought to be ineducable? Or perhaps it simply has to do with the fact that the main focus of attention, in educating a cat, is on telling it what *not to do*… and the traditional deterrent that training relies on is punishments which the cat finds incomprehensible.

It is exciting, to begin with, if we just take close look at the origin and deeper meaning of *education* in various languages. From the etymological point of view, the German word for it, *erziehen*, is connected with the Latin *educare*, to feed or nourish, as well as with *educere*, to bring forth. In an extended sense, then, we can see education as a bringing forth and a feeding –

which includes feeding with knowledge, of course. We can also see a hint in *educare* of the English *to care* – to look after someone, see to their needs or simply care for them. The German word *erziehen* is made up of pulling.

Taken all in all, training or education in this literal sense of the word has nothing – nothing whatsoever – to do with drill, discipline or pressure!

Educating means pulling, not pushing!

And based on that fundamental principle you can educate cats – and other animals as well, for that matter – very effectively and above all with complete success. The first step in the direction of successful feline education, then, is to do away with this restrictive idea of unlimited obedience (also in relation to *not doing*) and create a new and much more all-embracing picture of the *well educated* animal. This picture of feline education involves learning and teaching, conveying and understanding information, it is concerned with security and caring for your cat. The goal of educating a cat in this way is to put at the animal's disposal – and our own – an extended set of competencies for more effective communication. As a result, cats will acquire a better understanding of our human everyday life, in which they are so closely involved. It should give cats the possibility of dealing with human demands and expectations on the everyday level, along with the necessities of care and medical treatment, or at least coping with these things with a minimum of stress. Proper training should give cats greater psychological robustness and flexibility – partly in view of the fact that they can then rely on more reliable information from their human friend. This kind of educating should create a basis for understanding between two so very different species, human beings and cats – which works to the advantage of both.

Why should cats be educated?

Seen from this different angle, it gradually becomes clear that it makes a great deal of sense – and is in fact possible – to educate cats. Strictly speaking, practically all cats do undergo a certain fundamental education, even when it is not deliberately and actively instituted by human beings.

Basically speaking, there is no reason why cats should not be left as they have been brought up by their mother cats, if it were not for a major But…

In close cohabitation with human beings, and especially in conditions where the cat is completely without the possibility of roaming around freely, there are demands which are not so self-explanatory and obvious to cats as they are to humans. Left to themselves, cats will not have any particular interest in acquiring the relevant information, and actually will not have any way of doing so. They would simply go on being cats, just learning the things proper to a cat and nothing else – and in an independent cat's life, there wouldn't be any kind of problem about this.

But in close cohabitation with humans they need other, additional abilities – *life skills* (as Helen Zulch and Daniel Mills term them in their book for puppies) – in order to make it possible for the cat, in its relationship with its human, to live in a really relaxed, healthy and even happy way.

This starts right away with the cat's first car trip in a carrier, continues with the creative use of the bath mat instead of the cat's toilet provided and cheerful acrobatics on house plants or curtains, and often ends with the undesirable use of the dining table, giving pills, tooth cleaning or grooming. Misunderstandings between the two species, feline and human, are as common as their different needs. A good deal of disharmony and suffering on both sides could be avoided, if even just a few of the inter-species problems and barriers to understanding could be overcome.

The goal of feline education, then, is to enhance the life quality of the cat – but not at the expense of the cat's owners, who are so often willing to demote themselves to the status of 'tin opener' and servant, or practically the slave, of their cats. Living alongside human beings, and adjusting to their habits as opportunistically as possible, does not mean that the cat and the human really understand one another. At latest when you want something from some cats which they are unwilling to accept – and it may be something as elementary as letting you pick them up, grooming them, or giving them eye drops – the good relationship comes to an end. The cat suddenly gets scared and defends itself against the presumed predatory animal who is the human being, who has now taken on unpredictable and incomprehensible threatening traits. Mutual trust, fragile at best, is now well and truly cracked, and after a few more times when you stuff the cat in the transport box or give it pills the cat has definitely decided that this is no longer fun. Cats are really quick to learn, and will start to anticipate even the tiniest irregularity in everyday routine as the indication of potentially dangerous and certainly stressful human interference. In the worst case scenario, this interplay of cat and human can develop into a chronic state of anxiety, bringing in its train more and more problematic symptoms – house soiling, urinary marking, defensive aggression and even illnesses brought on by chronic stress.

Along with health and the sense of physical wellbeing, freedom from constant anxiety is an important aspect of life quality – and when the cat cannot even understand or make sense of everyday activities in its human environment, the avoidance of specific stress-related events, like visits to the vet, is not going to help much. Quite the reverse is the case – the less frequently a cat is put in its carrier, and experiences the in itself quite harmless handling of a veterinary examination, the greater its fear will be of these events which overshadow its peaceful and predictable everyday routine.

But vice versa, there can also be problems when cats want something, or need something, from us human beings. With breathtaking rapidity they learn what activities are going to enable them to reach their goal – and only in very rare cases will these be desirable patterns of behaviour. This is above all down to the fact that the learning process is a very one-sided affair, because the cat learns from its own success without our even having noticed what is going on. So when you come down to it, undesirable behaviour is most likely to deliver the goods, because it triggers the speediest reaction in human beings. Feline behaviour that is actually seen as desirable, on the other hand, will be regarded as normal and taken for granted – to such an extent that the cat is only really noticed when it does something inappropriate or forbidden.

The human-feline relationship is thus characterised by mutual incomprehension as well as by different needs, and can actually suffer seriously as a result. In the long term cat owners then resort to hopeless punishments, inducing anxiety in the cat, resign themselves or avoid the issue. Sadly this often ends with the cat being denied any medical care, attention and prophylaxis – either altogether, or at least for a very long time – because it results in *too much stress.* In the context of daily life, this means that cat owners feel themselves to be tormented and terrorised by their cats, because the animals seem *deliberately* to be peeing in the plant pots, meowing at the bedroom door or scratching the sofa. Or else the cat lives in a state of permanent insecurity, because although it can learn a lot of things, it cannot comprehend why it should be scolded for totally normal cat activities like scratching, peeing or communicating.

To sum up, we can say that educating a cat consists in
- encouraging and using their outstanding cognitive abilities,
- giving them information they can understand and positive feedback,
- extending their possibilities of expression and *life skills* in such a way that we can understand each other better in our living together,
- getting them to tolerate a necessary degree of manipulation,

- while at the same time guiding them in such a way that their needs and expectations are respected, so that the deal becomes a good and enriching exchange for both partners.

Taken all in all these are good reasons why we should take up the challenge, and educate cats in a deliberated way, proactively and following a specific plan.

It's a matter of creating a relationship

This active approach to educate your cat brings a whole bunch of practical benefits – and among them is a completely new, and essentially more intensive dimension in your relationship with your cat. This is because, in order to apply these techniques, you will have to observe your cat in a much more conscious way, from a quite different inner standpoint. You will need to look for the cat's motives and needs, and when it comes to clicker training, you will even be able to see how the cat is thinking. Even if you have known or had many cats in your life so far, when you engage in the proactive training of a young cat there is a high probability that you will experience a new kind of relationship and communication with your cat such as you never dreamed of before.

Educating cats is a challenge

Even though cats grasp things quickly and are speedy learners, educating a cat nonetheless remains in a certain sense a challenge. Cats do learn extremely quickly – in fact you might almost say that they learn too fast, for when they have once found out how to irritate us humans or produce a reaction, it will be more and more difficult to change the habits. So the important thing is to start the cat's education at the earliest possible stage!

And early, in this context, means thinking about it even before the cat arrives, being concerned with the cat's education and getting interactively engaged with it from the moment the cat arrives at your home.

For starters there is always a motivation, which will be examined more closely in a later chapter. Recognising what a cat wants, and what at this moment constitutes a reward for the cat, is first and foremost a learning process for us humans. Rewarding cats is in fact not always an easy thing – unless you have a very greedy *or* playful young cat. Or even better a greedy *and* playful kitten. The younger a cat is, the better the chance that you can find something which will easily get it excited, which represents fun and enjoyment for your kitten.

And likewise the opposite of rewards – punishing cats, that is – is as senseless as it is difficult. Direct punishment teaches cats one thing above all: *Do what you want, but only when no one is looking!* Yelling at them, squirting them with water and the various forms of physical punishment are incomprehensible to cats, damaging the relationship and the sensitive trust of the cat in the large animal that is the human being. The two typical reactions of the cat to punishment are flight or aggressive defence, in the best case scenario just ignoring it. Neither the one nor the other supports the desired learning process, because the information content of punishment for the cat approximates to zero. Meanwhile the cat's stress level goes into the red zone. Both factors are an obstacle to successful learning!

Cats, moreover, are not really team players, although of course they are thoroughly social animals. By contrast with dogs, they are not dependent on social structures in order to survive, and they do not need a team to overpower their small prey like mice. If a cat finds itself in a difficult situation, it will generally try to solve the problem on its own. Unlike dogs, it isn't typically going to turn to human beings for social support but will deal with the problem alone. Encouraging cooperation in certain situations, getting the cat to rely on human beings as a source of information, is one of the fundamental goals of educating cats, and in today's world represents an important life skill. With dogs this is practically something to be taken for granted – but with cats, it is something that has to be worked on and earned.

And finally we come to the biggest challenge of all in educating kittens – their persistence and endurance. What pitiful hunters they would be – in real outdoor life conditions, condemned to death by starvation – if they were to let themselves be discouraged by occasional setbacks or minor failures. A small reverse is not going to hold back any active, inquisitive and well-motivated kitten from doing something that actually does promise to be entertaining, exciting or delicious.

This also explains the recurrent sense of frustration when a cheerful young cat jumps onto the table for the umpteenth time, although it has been forbidden to do this umpteen times already. *It's not possible that it doesn't get the message!* The problem here is not necessarily the cat's obtuseness, but rather its exceptional level of performance, combined with high motivation when faced with a lack of any equally exciting alternatives. *Not on the table* definitely conveys too little information to have the right effect on its own!

There are two essential reasons why a cat will always go on making new attempts, with exceptional stubbornness and endurance, in order to reach its goals.

Either it needs something really urgently – though *need* here may well be a relative term, sometimes representing wanting rather than real necessity. Or else it rates its chances of getting what it wants as being after all quite high. Even the tiniest doubt on the human side is enough to encourage the cat to keep trying – *just keep at it for a while longer, and it will be in the bag.*

And secondly, cats have an easy time of it when we are not attentive – just a few successful experiences are so effective in confirming an attitude that it will last their whole life long.

So when a cat is tiresome, in the sense of tiresomely persistent, you should ask yourself the crucial question *What does the cat really want?* Cats generally are not tiresome just for the sake of being tiresome, but because they need (or want) something. And it is completely senseless trying to *teach* a cat in this kind of situation on the basis of just ignoring or punishing it for the sake of not letting it get away with anything! To begin with, this only ensures that the cat will be even more persistent – and secondly, to *educate* a cat means caring and providing, giving it information and not just ignoring it.

The great educational challenge, then, is to recognise what the cat needs – its motivation – and how to establish a controlled equilibrium between demanding and getting what it wants.

The true art of feline education is to make use of the cat's motivation and persistence, and steer it by suitable direction into acceptable channels.

Educating cats – won't it be terribly time-consuming?

Time is of course a very relative commodity – and what after all does a lot of time or a little time mean, in the context of cat education? Less time in comparison with educating kids – that is certainly the case, cats can be pretty well and truly educated in six months to a year! A lot of time in comparison with the way people have related to their cats in the past – again, that is a definite yes!

Carrying out the complete educational programme for kittens described in this book certainly calls for a much greater time investment than has generally been dedicated to the education of young cats in the past.

At all events it changes the *way* in which you spend time with a kitten in quite crucial respects – the relationship is more conscious, more attentive and very probably more understanding in the most literal sense!

> **If you see the education of a young cat, and the development of a heartfelt relationship, as a time commitment – in a sense suggesting the waste of time – such an attitude is liable to prompt the question whether you are willing to be a responsible cat owner in the first place…**

But what is a whole lot more important than the time involved is the undivided attentiveness and awareness that an active educational programme calls for!

Kittens need lots of small training units, each of them calling for just a few minutes, in some cases only seconds. These can easily be incorporated in the context of normal everyday activities. You just have to remember to do them!

It doesn't take a lot of time to invite a young cat to sit in the wish box, to involve the starting box in evening games or to call for a nose target from time to time so that the game will continue or remain under control.[1] Likewise quite normal forms of manipulation, like holding still, grooming, teeth cleaning or giving pills can be incorporated quite easily in everyday cuddle or play sessions – it only changes the nature and intention of the contact a little in an educational direction, to which positive feedback is added as information on a regular basis.

The exciting thing about educating a kitten – which actually makes it easy – is that for the most part it doesn't matter to the cat what learning games you play with it, as long as it all stays appetising, cheerful and friendly!

The real success in cat training will be when the little exercises happen in a quite automatic way as a part of your everyday routine, and *your* adult cat too comes to see the things it has learned as the most normal thing in the world – even if that still makes it stand out quite a bit from the crowd.

---

[1] Translator's note: these terms will be explained in detail later on.

Although the first six to ten months of an intensive programme of training call for a lot of input, in terms of time you remain independent and can carry out the greater part of the exercises at home – even the weekly excursions to other places can easily be integrated with the educational routine, in the form of a family visit or a trip to the vet.

But in any case it takes a certain amount of time and energy to focus on the cat's motives and motivation, to think up new things to attract its interest, to observe the cat or systematically involve varied learning routines in everyday situations.

For both humans and for cats, learning is fundamentally a process lasting the whole of a lifetime – it never comes to an end! And however much experience you have and however many cats you have known, there are always new aspects and refinements to discover.

It also takes an *inner* attitude of patience – the feeling that you have *all the time in the world* – when you are working with cats, even with active young cats. It is no accident that cats have a certain touch of the meditative – hectic events and headlong decisions are foreign to them, except in situations of crisis.

In observing your cat, learn to see these small pauses for reflection, moments of considered waiting in the course of a game, not as indifference and boredom but rather as meditation in an everyday context. There really are times where kittens don't want to cooperate – where they sit there and act as if they had never heard of a nose target, and just don't want to comply with an invitation to fulfil their part of the deal. Here it helps just to give the cat time – any kind of impatience or tensely raised expectations will only prolong the waiting phase.

And don't worry – feline upbringing works even if you only carry out a small part of the exercises, without adhering rigidly to the training plan – the effect of these little exercises is enormous!

The raw materials

In the nature of things, not all kittens have the same abilities when it comes to learning. As with children, there are lively kittens who are eager to learn, and then again there are ones who are a bit slower on the uptake, or who are perhaps just less motivated to learn what we want them to. Not all kittens have the same interests and talents – some like carrying toys around and learn quickly to fetch, others prefer climbing and jumping and are not so keen on keeping still, and others yet again are passionate about food and will learn amazing tricks just for a tiny treat. But all cats are able to acquire the most important fundamental concepts for living with us!

Two factors are mixed in with the individual personality of a kitten – genetics, and the environment. The two influences cannot easily be marked off from one another, as the genetic basis often provides only the potential for future development. Only the right influences from the environment at the right time – for example, based on an encouraging education in the first weeks and months of life – enable the cat's full potential to unfold.

One of the most important genetic factors is the breed. Cats have probably only been domesticated for around 9000 years in all – nothing like so long as dogs. And far and away most domestic cats today are still in the first phase of domestication, where animals live together with human beings and are used by them, but are not yet subjected to any kind of selective breeding through the choice and vetting of partners for procreation.

The first cat breeds came from the Middle East and the Far East, where the history of the cat's domestication actually takes its origin. These ancient cat breeds include the Persian, the

Siamese and the Burmese, the Abyssinian, the Egyptian Mau or Angora and the Turkish Van. But even for these, the intensive and selective choice of mates and deliberate development of the breed is only a few centuries old. Domestic cats remain free on the whole to choose their own partners, so that their gene pool still results in a colourful mixture of many different characteristics and survival skills, which do not always make cohabitation with the small predator that is the cat an easy matter.

This is because purebred cats are selected not just for optical features, such as fur colour and patterning, length of hair and physical build, but also more or less deliberately with a view to their friendliness to humans and social behaviour. Breeders are all the more eager to have offspring from a purebred cat when they are not just pretty and successful in cat shows, but are also open and friendly with people, good mothers and well socialised in living with other cats.

With some modern and exceptionally attractive cat breeds like the Bengal or the Savannah, however, interbreeding with wild species of small cats has again resulted in a sometimes explosive but certainly very demanding mixture of the domestic and the wild animal.

And although the genetic foundations are very important, they represent only one side of the equation. Even during the pregnancy countless forming environmental influences are already affecting the unborn kittens – like chronic stress on the part of the mother, for example, or dietary factors. The best genetic mix of a purebred cat will not give the animal a head start if it is exposed to unfavourable conditions and finds no soil in which it can flourish.

The second decisive factor for the cat's personality, then, is the environment – particularly during the first few weeks of life, when the kitten has experiences which will have an abiding and fundamental influence for the rest of its life. Nature's original idea was that a kitten who was scarcely formed in developmental terms, because blind and deaf, would be better able to adapt in a flexible way to its special environment by undergoing individual development subsequently. Well – this plan failed to take account of cases where kittens learn about life in the freedom of the farmyard and then move to a tiny city apartment on the fourth floor, where they come from an expansive Greek hotel garden to a terraced house estate, or from a female single household to the turbulence of a teaming patchwork family. Such fundamental changes in the living environment represent a major challenge even for the most adaptable kitten – sometimes an insuperable one...

These first few weeks of life in which the kittens are still living with their mother, siblings and perhaps even other adult cats in their original family are a very special, because *sensitive phase*. At this stage the kittens develop a reference system for their environment – they start to see, hear, taste and smell, and to move around the room.

From this moment on *everything* that they experience and perceive is at the same time learning for life – and the more they experience, the more they will learn. This is because the still immature brain develops in parallel to the sensory stimuli the kitten experiences, and so learns what in the environment is normal and what is dangerous. These initial impressions leave permanent and irrevocable traces which can no longer be modified in the course of the cat's later life, or can only be changed with a great deal of effort.

In principle cats would be inclined to see human beings as dangerous – as a large predatory animal – and only the learning process of the first seven weeks of life brings it about that the cat classifies humans as a friend and life partner rather than an enemy. Everyday encounters with the human environment – different sounds, activities of people coming and going, children running around, loud music, vacuum cleaning or everyday things like cat litter leave an important and abiding impression on the kitten.

So in selecting a young cat it is exceptionally important that it should have had as many positive experiences with different human beings and environmental influences as possible, because it will hardly be possible to make up for the lack of them subsequently.

So in summing up we can say that the more varied and rich in content the environment the kitten experiences, the better conditions it provides for later learning and life in close proximity with human beings.

Thus a young cat can become flexible, quick to learn and intelligent not so much because it is a particularly active pedigree cat, but rather because it has been challenged and encouraged by the human environment in the best possible way as early as in the first few weeks of life.

Depending on the degree of encouragement your kitten has received and its individual genetic predisposition, you should take its individual level as a point of departure for educating it and encouraging its further development.

With a not particularly well socialised kitten, the first steps of training may involve getting the animal to trust you and allow you to pick it up without stress; when the kitten is exceptionally well socialised, it may learn a perfect *Sit Pretty* in the very first hour of your acquaintance, willing to wear a harness and go for walks on a leash.

From the point where you take the kitten home, however, the same principle applies to all kittens – don't lose a single minute, get started with their education as quickly as possible!

The first learning process – socialisation

Strictly speaking, learning and training start for kittens from the moment when they come into the world. In these first few days of life the mother cat is the existentially crucial centre of their life – they suckle, are warmed and looked after. But it isn't just on the physical level that kittens are cared for by their mothers, there are also important developments on the emotional level. Chemical messenger substances – the *cat appeasing pheromone* – bring about an intensive bonding as the foundation for further learning processes. A stable and secure bonding makes the kitten more resistant to stress and enables it to make an early start with exploring the wide new world, because it can return at any moment to the familiar feel of its mother's tummy.

Cats are proverbially good mothers, and it is not surprising that the Egyptians reverenced them for that reason. But even for experienced and socially competent mother cats, bringing up and educating kittens is hard work – and how much more difficult does the job become when sources of food are scarce, the stress considerable and the dangers many and various!

As soon as the kittens start, at the age of three to four weeks, making their first attempts to crawl out of the nest into their immediate surroundings, the mother cat has her paws full – getting the kittens back into the nest, or carrying them back if they have gone too far; purring and chirping to keep up voice contact with them; and grooming them over and over again as a soothing activity.

Feline education starts right from the time when the mother cat pins down her kittens to groom them.

Cats in the wild start the weaning process at this age already, by refusing to let their young suckle and bringing them prey they have caught instead. As a result of this increasing rejection kittens not only become familiar with solid food, but also and more importantly learn to deal with frustration. It's true of cats as well – you can't always have everything you want at once!

Well fed mother cats who do not have to hunt for themselves naturally restrict suckling at this age as well, without of course being able to offer natural prey as a substitute. They then function as a model for imitation, and the kittens simply follow their mother to the feeding bowl.

Mother cats vary widely in relation to the weaning process. They may be very strict and consistent in weaning their young, or else extremely generous, letting their offspring who have practically reached the age of puberty continue to suckle alongside the next generation.

For a lurking predator like the cat, the frustration tolerance and impulse control learned in the course of weaning are a skill essential to survival. And these acquired skills are also quite crucial for cohabitation with human beings and communication with other cats!

In parallel to this process of education, which can last several weeks, young cats also learn the subtleties of social interaction with one another. This includes sending communication signals correctly and learning to understand the signals of others; avoiding, resolving or de-escalate conflicts; finding out how rough you can be without going so far that your siblings no longer want to play with you, or how polite you have to be if you want to be tolerated by an adult cat.

In this period the kittens also learn a whole lot of life lessons from their mother's example and by experimenting on their own account – for example, what things are good to eat, what materials are good for digging (so you can use them for a cat's toilet) and where you should hide in case of danger.

How do I choose a kitten?

The enormous importance of socialisation in the first weeks of life also shows how important the origin and selection of a kitten is! After all, you are going to be sharing your life with this animal in the best case for the next 20 years – so you are entitled to take a close look into the question whether you are well suited! In accordance with another philosophy, you could just take cats as they come, like children… You have the choice – or then again, perhaps you don't!

Along with the health criteria that generally need to be taken into account, when it comes to choosing a cat there are some patterns of behaviour which will give you clear indications as to what fundamental personality type your kitten belongs to:

- Self-confident, trusting, enjoying contact, friendly, unworried, relaxed
- Shy, timid, reserved, unapproachable, unfriendly, fearful
- Actively aggressive, defensive, rough, intolerant

If you have the choice and are able to look around for a new member of your family – from a breeder, from one or more different litters, or at the animal rescue home – it is good to know what is the important thing if you are to select the right kitten for yourself. One very important point – the colour is not that important!

But even if you acquire your new kitten without a whole lot of questions and premeditation, just as it comes, it can equally be helpful to know at what level you should start its education.

So the question is – what should a kitten, in the best case scenario, already be capable of, and how do you find out what it learned already?

Parents: the genetic foundations of the personality come from both the cat's parents – and you can most easily find out about them from the breeder. In the great majority of cases, however, only the mother cat is likely to be present. She is not just genetically important for the behaviour of her kitten, she is also its most important role model. If a mother cat shows herself to be open, self-confident and friendly, her behaviour will influence the attitude to life of her young. If she is fearful and reserved or even aggressive, even with the best educational strategy you will have difficulty in teaching the young cat a different kind of attitude.

Openness and familiarity: young cats who have had a sufficient amount of human contact will be interested in human beings. Sometimes it may take a few minutes for them to thaw completely, but then they are likely to play in a carefree manner, climb all over you and allow you to pick them up. It is almost a guarantee of an open and lively kitten that it is able, when you meet it, not just to hold its tail upright but to bent it forward right along its back.

Young cats who can bent their tail over their back are the perfect choice!

Kittens who hide or do not want to be touched have probably not been sufficiently socialised to human beings – they may get used to their humans, but they are unlikely to develop into extravert cats with an open attitude to life.

A kitten who on first contact spits, snarls or tries to scratch and bite finds human beings so threatening that it defends itself vehemently. But if a kitten snuggles up to your hand, purrs or even stays resting on you in a relaxed way, it has just the kind of trusting openness which holds out the best prospects of a satisfying life together.

Another good opportunity of getting to know a kitten is to observe it playing. Does it easily get drawn into playing with a toy, like a feather teaser or a mouse cat toy – or does it remain hesitant, or (even when eager) reserved and skittish? Or does it become a properly wild, growling carnivore the moment it has caught hold of its prey toy, prepared to defend it against all its siblings? Well socialised kittens can easily get involved in a game, and will be willing to relinquish their prey toy to a human being, even if they may in some cases need a bit of persuasion.

Trusting, well socialised kittens will stay relaxed when picked up.

Picking them up: well socialised kittens who are familiar with people will let themselves be picked up while remaining relaxed –

practically like little rag dolls, they will let their legs and their bodies go, because since the first day of their lives they have known that nothing is going to happen to them. Losing the floor from under their feet, without any control, is potentially threatening for a small animal like a cat, and if they have not learned that the big human predatory animal does such things, they will be frightened. These kittens become rigid, stretch out their legs and spread their claws, looking for something to hold onto, or start to struggle in panic. If you want relaxed cuddles and an animal you can carry around with you, they are probably not the best choice.

Holding still: well brought up kittens have already learned from their mother to keep still when she pins them down – for example, for grooming purposes, or as part of a social game. This so-called psychomotoric self-control – the ability to exercise self-control in a situation, both physically and emotionally – makes the life of a cat very much easier, especially in relation to its living with people. If you already have some degree of trust with the kitten, try to restrict it in a sitting position or quite gently lay it on its side and hold it down just slightly, so that it can't get up again. A well brought up kitten will have learned how to hold still – and as soon as it has done so for a brief moment, you can release it once more.

NB: on no account should this form of manipulation be a frightening experience for the kitten! If you don't feel quite sure about it, ask the person with whom the kitten is most familiar to hold it down briefly.

Holding by the scruff of the neck: another little exercise, which strictly speaking is just a continuation of the previous one: hold the kitten, using two or three fingers, by the scruff of the neck, in the same way as the mother cat carries it. Lift it up a bit, or if it is less than 8 to 10 weeks old you can lift it right off the floor for a few seconds. Here again it will show (and this has been confirmed, incidentally, by a study) whether subsequent life with this kitten is likely to be a rewarding experience. An emotionally stable kitten with good self-control will allow itself to hang on, pull its legs in and arch its back. Less than perfect impulse control, and even hyperactivity, will reveal itself in just a few seconds in the form of violent resistance, extension of the paws, struggles to get free and squealing. You look better for another kitten, if you want to have a cuddly, friendly animal – this kitten is unlikely to develop into a tolerant easygoing cat, or at least will need a great deal of educational training.

When picked up by the scruff of the neck, kittens with good self-control remain relaxed.

Control of biting and scratching: this is another ability which a kitten should learn in the first weeks and months. Its little pointed milk teeth and tiny sharp nails can't do a great deal of damage as yet, when they are roughly used in play – but it does hurt all the same! Above all when the kitten is playing with its siblings, or with the mother cat, it receives direct feedback when it is being too rough. At seven to eight weeks a kitten should already be capable of controlling the playful urge to bite – at latest at the point when someone says Ow! or squeaks. Vigorous biting or scratching in social contact – as opposed to when it is hunting a toy – in any case testifies to a certain lack of respect and uncontrolled roughness.

As with kittens this learning process is still going on, above all in relation to human beings, biting and scratching should never be provoked as a game. Whether a kitten is rough or not is something you can very quickly find out if you manipulate it or play with it for a bit. It is a good way of testing the kitten's tolerance and measuring the vigour of its defences, if you stroke it carefully on the stomach. Here there are basically just two types of cat. One kind of cat loves being stroked and tickled on the belly; the others decline emphatically, with the most vigorous biting and scratching, to refuse this invasion of their intimate regions – again, it is your choice!

NB: fingers should never be offered as a prey toy – otherwise it is quite possible that cats will have no inhibitions about trying to kill the supposed prey with all the resources at their disposal!

Coming when called: in most households with kittens there is a universal call at feeding time, with which the young ones can also be summoned. Observe whether the kittens all come together, or whether it is actually possible to call them individually and whether they do in fact come.

Taking food from the hand: for a kitten it is not automatic to be able to take food from the hand. Without a certain learning process, they will either bite in an uncompromising manner, being unable to distinguish between the treat and the finger – or they will just not take the food, only taking note of it when they can see it on the floor in front of them. Although this ability is not all that important, it can be quite useful in subsequent training.

Grooming: long-haired kittens should definitely have had some experience of grooming from the breeder – even if their coat is still short and fluffy, and so easy to look after.

Social skills: relating to its mother, siblings and in the best case to other adult cats as well teaches the kitten how to behave politely. Kittens have an instinctive knowledge of the basics of feline communication – a simple and basic repertoire of cat language should at any rate be within their grasp. But when it comes to the subtleties of expression, of conflict resolution and appeasement, friendly de-escalation rather than symmetrical escalation, they will need to learn a whole lot more in addition to their inborn social streak. The standard eight weeks in their original family are hardly likely to be enough! So if you are looking for a young cat with well developed social skills, then you should allow it 12, or even better 16 to 20 weeks of educational and training time in its social cat group.

Social skills include the appeasement gesture of turning the head and look the other way in a conflict situation.

However nearly all of the behaviour patterns described may have to do with emotional and physical self-control –

a kitten who has been well habituated to people and brought up by a good mother cat should easily be able to handle all these forms of manipulation without anxiety. This psychomotoric self-control is the basis for all further learning!

Is there an ideal time for adopting a kitten?

Traditionally it remains the case, and is standard practice with the kittens of domestic cats, to separate them from their mother and adopt them in their new home at around the age of eight weeks. The kittens will then appear at first glance to be quite independent – they will eat on their own, use the litter box and play crazy games, while the mother cat often withdraws and may keep the kittens at a distance – sometimes even quite emphatically. And although these little eight-week-old cats are already capable of finding their feet in a new home, either on their own or with a sibling, the mother has by no means completed their education. Even if she only visits them a few times a day, the teaching is still continuing as a result of the role model effect – in what concerns communication, hunting and the gradual emotional detachment from the mother.

As we have already said, it actually takes very much more than eight weeks for the kittens to become socially competent, and many of our domestic cats suffer a more or less conspicuous handicap in relation to social forms of expression and relationships with other cats as a result of the early separation.

If kittens are only separated from their original family at 12 weeks or later, they can cope with the change and the many new experiences considerably better – though the difference only becomes clearly visible on the basis of a direct comparison.

On the other hand, young cats aged eight to ten weeks – shortly after the end of the first intensive socialisation phase, that is, which lasts up to the seventh week – are still open, inquisitive and willing to take on board all kinds of new things without a problem. The sudden loss of mother and siblings makes them very dependent, so that they quickly develop an affectionate relationship with their new person.

Especially when the mother has been very fearful, frightened of human contact or just unable to cope with the burden of motherhood, it may sometimes be better in the individual case to separate a kitten from her at an early stage. These kittens will then need particularly extensive positive socialisation from the first day – ideally with a sociable adult cat who can continue their education.

A study on the temperament of cats has shown that the personality scores of kittens remain quite stable approximately from the twelfth week. So with a kitten at the age of 12 weeks it is fair enough to say that *what you see is what you get*.

If the kitten you have chosen is open, friendly and self-confident at the age of 12 weeks, these basic traits are going to continue. If, on the other hand, it is shy, timid, intolerant and unfriendly, then it is unlikely to develop into an approachable and self-confident cat subsequently.

- If a young cat has grown up under good or ideal circumstances, 12 to 16 weeks are a good time to take it into your home.
- If conditions have been less than optimal or inadequate, adoption at the age of 8 weeks is still an acceptable time.
- Younger kittens should be separated from their mothers only in a real case of emergency.

When do you start educating a cat?

For feline education, there is one quite simple rule – the earlier, the better. Young cats are collecting new experiences all the time, and in early months they are still open and curious enough to experience a great deal, because it is part of their natural programme to learn a lot as fast as possible.

At latest from puberty, around the age of six months, it becomes more difficult, because by the time the cat becomes an adult it already has a much clearer idea of what it wants to do and what it does not want to do – and this in many cases will include the things it has not learned and has not experienced in the first weeks. The carefree, playful inquisitiveness of the extended sensitive phase now gives way increasingly to a critical or hesitant, sometimes even fearful aloofness and caution. Many cats start to become a bit wary at this age, and may turn out in certain circumstances to be insecure for the first time, or anxious in unfamiliar situations. So it is important to make use of every minute before puberty, and to make an early start – right from the first minute, that is to say, when you have your cat.

Or actually even earlier – because you should have already been thinking well in advance about what you want to teach your cat, and what will be the few real taboos that you are determined to insist on in all circumstances. You should also picture how much mischief one or two young cats are capable of getting up to – although the human imagination can never extend so far! And you should probably be considering and planning how to divert and attract the cat's typical and unavoidable activities – the ones you cannot really prohibit – into acceptable channels.

What is a well educated cat?

The object of successful feline education is a cat that in some sense is *well-behaved*, even though having a 'good' cat – one who obediently carries out orders – is unlikely to strike most cat owners as a desirable target to aim for. Cats are loved for their independence, for their love of freedom and also for their high measure of incorruptibility. This is all very well, but only until the point where a cat decides to pull out all the stops of stubbornness, creativity and persistence in order to do something it likes doing or that appeals to its curiosity – for preference, in the early hours of the morning. At latest when a half-grown cat jumps on the dining table for the 233rd time in order to see if there is something exciting there, your enthusiastic admiration of feline independence and curiosity will have reached an all-time low – and the idea of having a good cat, one who doesn't do one thing or the other when told not to do so, comes to appear increasingly attractive.

In everyday life this often results in a certain discrepancy between the independent fantasy image that hovers in the mind's eye, and what the cat actually does with our furniture.

The path to a good cat, then, starts from a sensible definition, which might for example be formulated on the following lines:

> A well-behaved cat is balanced, and indeed happy, because it has everything that it needs as a cat and so is able to come to an accommodation with the human environment in which it lives. An educated cat is not tiresome because it has learned to communicate what it needs, and its needs are respected and above all noticed right from the start. A good cat doesn't cause any damage – or only causes a limited amount – because it has been given the possibility, based on learning, of acting out the habits of behaviour typical of the species in a suitable manner. Or something similar…

Feline education can never mean making a cat into a *non-cat* – in the sense that it refrains from demonstrating behaviour which is after all natural to the cat.

Even a well-behaved cat always remains a cat!

All a question of motivation

Why do cats do what they do – and above all, the things you don't want them to do?

Every kind of behaviour has its motivation, and an approximate inkling or idea of why a cat does something can be very helpful when you want, as part of your course of training, to *steer* the cat in a different direction.

Fundamentally cats do not have a concept of *should* and *shouldn't*. They do things because they are the important thing at the time – for the most part, in terms of their own priorities.

Before you interpret an undesirable behaviour in the wrong direction – malice, jealousy, bloody-mindedness, protest – you should work through a checklist of simpler and more obvious motives in order to see whether they don't offer a more suitable explanation, which can then be dealt with much more easily by applying the principles of education in an extended sense.

…, because it's a cat

Many kinds of behaviour, in the cat's eyes, are quite simply the most normal thing in the world. This means that sometimes it is enough just to be a cat in order to do something – you don't need any further reasons. Strictly speaking this applies as a fundamental principle for all kinds of feline behaviour – they behave this way, because they are cats. The difficulties arise when we, as human beings, expect that cats should behave in the way we envisage from our human perspective, or in accordance with our human system of values.

This includes, for example, a number of problems that are frequently misunderstood – like scratching the furniture, early morning phases of activity, house soiling and urine marking.

A young cat pees on the blanket because it needs to pee *this minute*, and the blanket – as a large, soft and absorbent substrate – seems the perfect location to do so. Of course it knows the way from the bedroom on the first floor to the cat's toilet in the basement lobby, but in this situation it is too far to go and the blanket – conveniently – fulfils exactly the same purpose. Why can the cat go from the first floor to the kitchen for food, but not to visit the litter box? Because the cat cannot create an alternative feeding station of its own – but when it is a toilet that is required, it can solve the problem quite simply itself by finding a new place to pee in.

There are some kinds of behaviour which are undesirable but typical of the species – and here there is no possibility of finding an alternative in the form of 'not doing it'. The only possibility of changing the cat's behaviour is education whereby the cat is diverted or *steered*, right from the first day, towards more acceptable locations or objects.

..., because it's fun!

Above all for young and adolescent cats, many activities come with an extremely high fun factor. Behaving like a mad thing, rampaging around and trying out new things are quite simply central to the play activity of adolescent and young adult cats. When young cats want to experience the effect of their own activities and exercise their physical abilities, this can sometimes have deleterious implications for house plants, curtains or other furnishings. The curtain becomes a jungle creeper, challenging the cat to a daily test of daring – and why after all shouldn't the yucca palm be a climbing tree? Rattling materials, things that are in any way breakable, are just irresistible playthings for young cats. And yes, of course – when there's two of them, it is a whole lot more fun!

Punishment is no use, in the face of this high fun factor of playful learning. The only remedy is prevention! Sensitive and breakable objects which are unlikely to survive the cat's youthful phase, which are valuable or important to you, should just be put out of the way, locked up – or else written off and replaced.

..., because it's hungry.

Cats like a lot of small snacks, and in their active phases young cats are practically always looking out for food. Then too, in the first few months of life they are also open to learning what things are suitable as food, where you can be sure of finding them and how best to get at them. In life in the wild, this would be an extremely important learning process for the cat, crucial to its survival – and you can't just expect to turn it off because the cat is now living indoors and gets its food in a bowl. Exceptionally interesting places where the cat has excellent chances of finding food are at the same time often designated taboo zones, where the cat's presence is undesirable – rubbish bins, the dining table, the kitchen dresser... It's a major dilemma, because young and hungry cats above all are very highly motivated to get at these exciting food sources. And then there are the times when the cat strikes lucky – when it finds a leftover crumb or discovers the lingering remnants of an interesting scent – and pushing the cat down will weigh little in comparison with this sense of pleasant surprise! Hunger, however, is far and away the best motivation to educate a cat into alternative forms of behaviour.

..., because it needs something.

Need is always a relative term – and when we take a closer look, we human beings don't really need as many things as we suppose. Sometimes *need* is more the *desire to have*, just a subjective priority rather than something essential to life. It is reasonable to presume that cats too occasionally need something which simply serves for the satisfaction of a momentary impulse, in the sense of something they *want*. Indoor cats above all can do little to shape their lives for themselves, and so more frequently need something from us humans – apart from food, this also includes attention and entertainment, for example, as well as interactive play and cuddles. The more urgently a cat needs something or the higher it rates its chances of getting it, the more stubborn – or irritating – it will be in its demands. Just like hunger, this offers excellent motivation for educational purposes – but it does mean you really have to be willing to give the cat your undivided attention.

..., because it's curious.

Healthy cats are proverbially inquisitive, and this applies all the more to young cats, who are still eager to learn and are collecting new experiences on a daily basis. Not all cats jump into areas that are out of bounds because they are hungry – at least as strong a drive is curiosity, the wish to be close to the action. For a cat, our human contact zone – the face – is more often than not impossibly far out of reach, and what could be a more obvious way of resolving the problem than by meeting half way, on a table or some other raised surface? Adult cats as well are inquisitive observers, and like to be involved and watch when human beings are working on something. Observing is both an entertaining occupation for cats, and a social activity. It can never be the object of education to suppress or thwart this curiosity. Letting a cat participate in activities as an observer strengthens the relationship, and with education you can simply allocate the cat to its secure seat in the front row.

..., because it is ill.

Some misunderstood or undesirable patterns of behaviour in cats have a more serious background – because they feel unwell, or are actually suffering from an illness. Cats can be a little idiosyncratic in the way in which they communicate their physical discomfort, but in general their preferred strategy is to keep a low profile. This applies particularly to routine habits, gestures and forms of expression – not however to more conspicuous patterns of behaviour like house soiling, urine marking or chewing textiles. Whenever a cat does things that cats do not normally do, then it is reasonable to suspect that it has a physical problem. Educational measures will be useless here, but experienced handling makes it easier to examine and treat the cat properly.

..., because it's frightened.

Along with physical discomfort, emotional imbalance is an important reason for some kinds of behaviour – and in the eyes of the cat, it may even be a matter of existential importance. A cat naturally reacts with fear in many situations, because while it is a small predator, and capable of defending itself, it is itself a prey to larger predators. And one such large predator, in the cat's view, is the human being. Along with flight and hiding, self-defence is the second important strategy for fearful cats. Conventional training which merely defines itself on the basis of *Cats mustn't act like that*, and doesn't provide any effective opposite pole in information terms or any reliable positive feedback, is potentially fear-inducing. First of all, punishment will cause fear when the cat is doing something that cats just normally do; and what is worse, the individual encouragement and understanding you are aiming for has been lost along the way.

Certainly there are numerous other reasons why cats behave as they do; but if you are familiar with these seven types of motivation, that is easily enough for everyday training purposes with a young cat. In addition, not all cats are alike – some are greedy, and others are not so much interested in food; there are curious and playful cats who are capable of surprising you every day with their new ideas of what constitutes a game, and there are ones who are quiet and sedate and would never dream that there are any levels in the kitchen other than the floor; there are anxious young cats who are ready at any time to lie on their backs and defend their lives with claws and teeth, and there are friendly and self-confident kittens who have total trust in their humans in any situation.

And just as cats have different motivations, so the expectations of cat owners are equally varied. There are generous and tolerant people who like sharing their bed, table and ham sandwich with a cat, and there are restrictive ones who have a long list of things cats must not be allowed to do; there are empathetic ones who can imagine relatively easily what is important to a cat, and thoughtless ones who see cats as being simple and low maintenance, until the first misunderstandings about their needs start to emerge.

So feline education is always a process of learning and understanding *for both sides* and considering and familiarising yourself with these forms of motivation is a first important step towards steering the cat in the right direction.

The feline household – creating an environment to be good in

The first thing in educating cats is to offer them an environment where they can live out the behaviour typical of the species, without however conflicting with human living requirements. A certain degree of compromise is necessary here, obviously, and if you expect a cat to adapt 100% to human standards and conditions, you had better think again – with a real life cat.

Indoor only cats, generally speaking, have very few possibilities of improving their daily lives in the interest of satisfying their feline needs – they are entirely dependent on humans for this. But whenever cats try to improve their lives in a creative way, there is a major risk that their good ideas will meet with human disapproval.

In view of the loss of exciting possibilities of hunting, observation and exploration outdoors, an indoor existence will all too often leave cats deprived of any opportunity of planning their day in an exciting or relaxing way to suit their fancy. So human beings and a good social relationship with their humans become a more important factor for variation in the cat's life – one that is actually crucial to life quality. For the indoor cat, you might say that adventures outdoors have been traded in for the adventures of a human relationship. In order for this to work, to make it an acceptable bargain at the very least from the cat's point of view, the relationship with the human person must of course be very affectionate, and based on a fundamental understanding of the cat's nature. Cats are proverbially curious animals, so learning new things offers a possibility of mental stimulation even when there is an almost total lack of stimuli, variation or information from the natural environment outside.

All this entails a certain obligation to generosity, as well as to conscientious training – and responsibility for this lies quite definitely with the human being!

But even independent free-ranging animals with a cat door, for the reasons referred to above, will only derive benefit from the arrangement when human beings accept the responsibility – and at the same time the challenge – of educating them actively in addition.

So with an appropriate cat-friendly domestic environment, you offer cats right from the start basic conditions which make *being good* an easy matter. Although there certainly are some cats answering to the traditional view that they are simple, uncomplicated and undemanding pets who can be left on their own for hours or even for a whole weekend, and then used for cuddles in the evening, this will be quite untrue of a great many cats!

This applies all the more in that human beings' expectations of the cat, as a companion and emotional addition to their own life, have risen, while at the same time the freedom of the cat is reduced by its being kept indoors.

The most important environmental resources for cats – like food, water and a litter box – seem at first glance to be obvious. But the expectations typical of the species are not always that easy to meet by any means, and some of their behavioural patterns frequently result in misunderstandings.

Feeding

Practically all cat owners spend a lot of thought on the *what* of feeding – the cat food should of course be a good quality one, and if you love your cat, you will be happy to offer it more exclusive varieties. Particularly important to the diet of kittens (as well as pregnant mothers) are certain special fatty acids, like DHA (docosahexaenoic acid) and EPA (eicosapentaenoic acid). The brain consists for the most part of fat. When the kitten, who is born as a half-finished product so to speak, has a ready source of top-quality building materials for its brain in the first few months, clearly more effective hardware will also develop for the software that you aim to install in the form of education.

But if in feeding cats you only focus on criteria like dry food vs. wet food, high-value sources of protein, fatty acids, low cereal content and freedom from additives, you are still far from consulting the cat's best interests!

No less important – especially for the emotional wellbeing of the cat – is the *how* factor. And seeing that overweight, and the resulting chronic state of inflammation in the organism, has increasingly developed into one of the biggest health problems for cats today, the question of *how* is also connected with the question *how much* the cat should eat, or should be allowed to eat. Along with the cat's wellbeing, all this has a quite considerable effect on the cat's good behaviour and the success of education.

Offering cats, like dogs, just two or three meals a day is of course a practical solution, and almost normal practice, but it is hardly in keeping with their natural eating habits. Giving cats an unlimited amount of high-quality tasty dry food is also common, and is a good route to an overweight or obese sick cat.

Cats are actually snack eaters with a very small stomach, and they prefer 10 to 20 very small meals spaced out through the day and night. This results in a gap of one to three hours between meals, which are however quite small. A mouse, which in some case will not be eaten up completely, might have approximately 30 calories – and all in all, an average 4 kilogram (8,8 lbs) cat needs only something like 200 calories per day. A cat that looks after itself would then have to invest quite a lot of working effort in the form of hunting to obtain its food. When you add it all up, this amounts to 20-25 calories for 8 to

10 small meals at intervals of two or three hours. In practical terms, that would be roughly speaking around 5 to 10 kibbles or 10-30 grams (0,35- 1 oz) of wet food per meal.

It doesn't look like much – but the most effective diet for cats consists in a lot of small portions.

Then there is the fact that the cat prefers to eat freshly caught prey; and here its exceptionally sensitive perceptive capacity for sensing the start of decomposition helps it to decide on whether or not something is edible. Food residue that has been quietly going bad in the bowl for two hours or more will be seen by many cats as carrion, and no longer good to eat! This has the consequence that a feeding system that is to some degree cat-friendly cannot manage without dry food – unless a lot of work is going to be involved – if we assume that you are going out to work. Wet food or fresh food goes off far too quickly, and no longer meets the cat's standards of freshness – though it may still appeal to the flesh-flies…

These typical cat's needs give rise to some of the commonly misinterpreted patterns of behaviour and problems in the cat's sharing its life with human beings, as well as with other cats:
- Cats beg for food every few hours.
- They even do so, when there is still food in the bowl.
- Cats are demanding in the early hours of the morning, because they are hungry.
- Cats jump on the table and dresser in search of food.
- Hunger leads to frustration and harassment of other cats.
- Hungry cats eat too much at once and too fast, and overstep their satiety signal.
- Cats vomit soon after eating.
- Hunger is chronic stress.

All these problems can very often be attributed to a well-meant and indeed high-quality, but from the ethological angle not really cat-friendly restrictive system of twice daily feeding. The supposed educational effect when the cat is made to adhere to set feeding times, to discourage naughtiness, very often has precisely the opposite result – and it is a matter of need here, not of the cat's being tiresome or refractory.

The main pillars of a high-quality cat diet should therefore be supplemented, from the time when the cat is quite young, with a few essential aspects which also have educational implications:
- Cats should be given access to small amounts of food every few hours.
- All, or at least a part of the food should call for a certain expenditure of effort and time – either in the organisation or in the eating.

In a nutshell – there won't be dry food served in a bowl at all, it will only be given as a working meal or as *activity feeding.*

This way young cats learn right from the start that they can always count on being allowed access to food, and don't have to bolt down huge portions as if they were starving twice a day – with the result that they overstep their natural satiety signal, and may be sick soon after eating. They learn likewise that they have a certain autonomy and responsibility on their own account for acquiring their food, so that boredom during the day is counteracted by a highly meaningful activity, and there is less chance of their becoming overweight. And finally, their learned independence in getting their food can be a crucial advantage when the cat, as an early riser who favours the twilight hours, starts to feel hungry for the first time at four in the morning.

Feeding cats is thus an individually adapted strategy, consisting of regularly dispensed small portions and food that the cat itself has to work for.

Although this strategy is very much easier to implement with dry food, when you have plastic utensils that are easy to clean you can also offer wet food as a working meal.

Less intensive hunger phases and cat-friendly meaningful activity encourage inner contentment – which is *the* essential foundation for a well-behaved happy cat!

The possibilities of cats' working meals are many and varied, and here again variation is desirable – essentially this forms part of the educational plan, as it keeps the cat flexible and extends its horizons. Not all the possible options will necessarily be to the cat's or the owner's taste, and depending on the cat's motivation, eagerness and tendency to put on weight, the level of difficulty should also be gradually adapted to the cat's capabilities and willingness to tolerate frustration.

- Activity feeding: Pipolino, NoBowl Feeding System, Kong, Wobbler Kong, Cat Pyramid, Dog Brick, Dog Tornado, Buster Activity Mat, commercially available or homemade cat activity boards, foraging boxes, silicon baking trays for small muffins, egg boxes, food in small bowls, in paper bags or under cups, plastic bottles or small cubic storage boxes with holes, etc.

Windy Whisper and Fiji File working together to get their food out of the Cat Pyramid

Windy Whisper fumbling the Dog Tornado

Fiji File learned at an early age how to work for his food.

*Sunnyboy has already learned how to use his teeth
in the way proper to a cat for big pieces of meat.*

- Offer meat in increasingly larger pieces (depending on taste, either raw or cooked) which the cat has to break down using its back teeth: e.g. beef pieces for goulash, chickens' hearts, raw chicken necks, turkey hearts, dried meat etc.
- Offer food in small jam or dessert bowls as one-off snacks, varying the spot.
- Offer whole animals: one-day-old chickens (possibly deep frozen), mice or rats.
- Incorporate food in exercise modules, e.g. get the cat to earn its food as a part of clicker training.

But the learning and training process for young cats not only involves the realisation that they have to do something to earn their meals – they also need to experience as many different types of food as possible. Here it is not just a matter of different tastes – the important thing is the consistencies and the textures, as well as the various shapes and sizes of kibbles, raw or cooked meat (no raw pork), wet food in the form of bits with gravy, compact in jelly or the various consistencies of cat's pâté supplied by commercial manufacturers. Kittens learn from their mother what is edible, and generally remain quite open to new experiences of food for the first few months of life.

But in addition to this, there is a technique involved in the eating of large pieces of meat or prey animals, and this can only be acquired through experience. Gnawing big pieces of meat with the back teeth is a very sensible feed strategy from the point of view of dental health, and it is essential that cats learn how to do it. At the time of the change of teeth, between four and seven months, it is quite possible that young cats will be unwilling or unable to bite big pieces of food, or else quite the reverse, they will show a predilection for gnawing.

If new kinds of taste, varieties of food or treats fail to awaken the cat's interest, mixing the new element in with the food the cat is familiar with is the simplest way to add new items to its horizon of experience. All the same, tastes are individual, and there will be cats for whom it is not a matter of experience and habituation – they really do just dislike something, if they consistently reject what is offered them.

If you bring up young cats with this feeding technique from the start – reliable access to food in very many, very small portions, keeping things interesting by making the cat work for it, even if this takes some time – there is less need to prohibit unwanted behaviours linked to hunger. Even if castrated cats later on do experience some hormone-based adjustment to the metabolic system, this strategy is still the simplest way of avoiding overweight problems.

Water supply

Water in motion from the cat's drinking fountain is entertaining for many kittens, and makes a highly attractive water resource.

Water availability is hardly seen as important in connection with cats – it is one of those areas of behaviour that is just noticed but not really perceived. And yet we so often hear complaints either that cats won't drink at all, or that they use all possible sources of water except the one intended for them. In terms of life quality and health, and also in an educational sense, the supply of water can actually be a very important factor. As former desert dwellers, cats are not generally inclined to drink a great deal, and absorb a large part of their water needs through their food. But if dry food bulks large in the cat's diet, it is essential to provide a variety of attractive sources of water.

Kittens all have their first learning experiences sooner or later with saucers of milk or water, sticking their noses in the liquid and then sneezing. This is because cats do not actually see the surface of the water right in front of them, and have to learn a tactic for judging the distance correctly so as to be able to drink without accidentally dipping their noses.

One of these techniques is to dip in their paw – either directly in the saucer, so as to lick the water off the paw, or by stirring up the water so that it is easier to see the surface of the liquid.
Many cats look for more pleasant water sources than the perfectly clean, crystal-clear drinking bowl, which makes it difficult for them to drink in a relaxed way. Flower pots, watering cans, drinking glasses, water-filled pans in the sink are all popular, and surfaces wet with water like the shower tray, bath tub or indoor fountain are also a welcome resource for the cat. There is nothing against this in principle, but it makes more sense to offer the cat suitable water resources right from the start, which will always actually be available and can more easily be monitored. Occasional variation in the type and location of the water will increase the cat's flexibility, as well as its water intake – open-minded cats are happy to try out something new, and will only hold onto their temporary preferences until such time as they discover a new preference.

Cats with a passion for water like playing with drinking vessels, and will soon have the entire area around their bowls under water. Water in motion is very much more entertaining than standing water, and exercises a quite special fascination on many cats – especially when it disappears down the drain. If it is not in motion, cats will dip their paws in it, try to chase reflections or fish out small objects from below the surface. If you have a water-obsessed young cat like this, you would do well to offer it a water play station from the start, before it starts looking for its own. Water in the bath tub, small basins of water – on the balcony in summer, say – with floating animals, cork disks, ice cubes and the like, can even be used as entertainment in the context of activity feeding, so as to get the cat working for its food.

In an educational sense it is useful to know that smart cats are quick to learn that by asking for water they can launch a quite special programme of entertainment. These cats prefer flowing fresh water direct from the tap – and the attention that they receive in addition, in this situation, when they claim to be thirsty again. If you see the activity as a game, this is not a problem – but it is essential that the cat should learn that it can access water independently.

Possibly you should try out different sorts of drinking fountain – water can be in the form of surface wetting or a free jet, can well up or flow either quickly or slowly – because not all cats like all kinds of fountain.

Here are some ideas for a cat-friendly water supply:
- In principle keep water apart from the feeding station.
- Based on your living space, provide several water sources.
- Offer different qualities of water – water in motion in the cat's fountain, and standing water in the bowl.
- Try out different water bowls, wide ones and narrow ones; darker vessels are preferable, with a visible limescale border.
- Try out different locations and different lighting conditions, making it easier for the cat to see the water surface.
- Always fill water vessels up to the brim.

- Objects that break the surface of the water make it easier for the cat to detect – for example a stone, water plants or an anti-gulp dog bowl.

Litter box

Here's the good news: kittens do not have to learn from us how to use a litter box – they already know instinctively what it is all about, if you introduce them to your home at the standard age of eight – or better, twelve – weeks. But this does not automatically mean that it is always going to stay that way for the rest of their lives…

One of the commonest problems – above all with young cats – is their inquisitive liking for experiment, coupled with the fact that often too few litter boxes are made available in comparison with the living space. From the point of view of a young cat who is used to playing or sleeping on the bed, what reason is there not to try out this beautifully soft and absorbent quilt as a toilet, when the only box provided is so far away in the bathroom or a story further down in the basement? The knowledge is there, admittedly, but the motivation of a young cat will not always be sufficient to make it travel the long distance to the cat's toilet, if there are alternatives readily available.

Sometimes it seems quite astonishing – but cats really do, for the most part, use the toilets they are offered. But this cannot be taken for granted with every cat, and without regard to all the circumstances. And then there is the fact that the cat's needs relating to the toilet may change when it becomes an adult or grows older, so that what a fit young cat may find to be OK will be regarded as rather less than optimal, or even out of the question, by a grown or mature cat. When we see this in terms of the much shorter life stages of a cat, it may well be the case that its preferences and needs in relation to the litter box will change in the space of just a few years.

A spacious adventure toilet with fine litter is the best plan for preventing house soiling.

The best idea is to head off the cat's creative search for an alternative place to do its business by providing the kitten right from the start with irresistible and ample adventure toilet facilities. This may include:
- at least two different locations, away from feeding places,
- free and unhampered accessibility at all times,
- generous size, so that adult cats can still turn around and dig *comfortably* in the tray or box,
- quite fine-grained and clean, but unscented and low-dust litter, ideally one that forms solid clumps,
- without a lid, though the sides may of course be higher (with a lower access point if necessary).

Cats cannot be compelled to approve of a litter box which conforms to our human expectations – they have their own ideas how a good cat's toilet should look, and where it should be located – and they may stick to their views with great consistency. Cats are not all the same, either, in their high expectations or willingness to compromise – just as with human beings, some cats are compulsive cleanliness fanatics and others are less fussy, more capable of dealing with mess and muckiness.

Very young kittens have a tendency, on their first visits to the litter box, to try to eat the litter – so with very young kittens, a non-clumping litter is safer in the early stages, to avoid problems with constipation. As soon as they have acquired some experience with the toilet, a fine clumping litter is the sensible solution that best answers to the cat's needs.

Habituation is actually an extremely important basic learning process for the cat – the longer it goes on using a specific spot as its toilet, the more consistently it continues to do so. With house soiling cats the important thing is to react immediately, before the new place it has picked on establishes itself as a habit, because it is in any case more convenient than the postage-stamp-sized cat toilet provided in the furthest corner of the utility room.

Depending on the animal's sensitivity, you can certainly give your cat carefully chosen rewards for using the litter box and teach it a word for it, at your discretion – but you would do best to contact the cat only when it is already finished and is digging in the litter. Decency and respectful distance can be taken for granted in this case – a quiet *click* or a twinkling nod to show your appreciation (*I saw what you did*) are enough as positive feedback – followed by a small treat or a play, as a real reward, if that is what the cat wants. It is not in itself necessary to reward the cat for urinating – the emptying of the bladder is already a reward – but you should confirm that the place is the correct one and teach the cat a word for it. When the cat has learned the word, you can then quite easily invite it to use the litter box before it is taken on a long road trip.

If you make short excursions to new places with your kitten, it is sensible to have a small *litterbox to go* on hand. An ordinary household plastic box with lid, filled with clumping litter, which you can always take with you is sufficient for the purpose. Whereas grown cats can hold out for several hours without any problem, after two exciting hours small cats with an active metabolism are likely think another visit to the toilet is already called for!

Scratch marking facilities

Cats need a scratching post, then they will leave the furniture alone. Well, yes and no – with scratching and marking too, successful education consists in a combination of facilities that appeal to the cat's needs and a learning process as backup support.

A single scratching post can meet all a cat's needs – though it doesn't have to – even if it is beautifully designed with pillars of natural wood and as high as the ceiling. The important thing is to understand *when, where and why* cats scratch the furniture in the first place.

Apart from the fact that it is something that cats just do, further motives may include the following:
- Marking resting places and retreats with pheromones – like the arm of the sofa, which is a place for sleeping and resting; the carpet next to the cat's bed, or the yucca palm by its cosy den.
- Working off excitement, frustration or tension – for example when hungry; happy excitement when saying hello, playing, petting; stress with other cats or people, or general dissatisfaction with the current state of things.
- Boredom, because many cats – unfortunately – learn that they can count on getting the immediate attention of their humans if they scratch in places that are strictly forbidden.
- A side-effect of scratching is spinal extension and stretching, as well as care of the claws – neither of these, though, need necessarily involve the destruction of surfaces as they can happen anywhere else.

It follows, then, that you will almost always have to offer more than just one scratching area in order to divert these different scratching motives towards suitable and desirable spots. These strategically placed scratching facilities do not necessarily have to be ceiling-high or exceedingly big – it's enough if they are just there, as a practical scratching opportunity. But the cat's material preferences can be very individual, and are very likely to be influenced by the animal's previous experience.

Scientific studies have found the following characteristics in scratching facilities to be favourable to the needs of most cats:

- Approximately one meter (40 in) high, and not too broadly based – a pillar, in other words. Alternatively, a scratching post in diagonal or even horizontal alignment can be provided.
- Sisal and other natural fibres, carpet and even tight rolled corrugated cardboard are seen as a good scratching accessory by the great majority of cats. Some specialists however tend to favour soft wood, or even plastic materials.

As a general principle, if a scratching post is offered from the first day in the right location, in most cases it will be well accepted.

Along with an attractive range of scratching boards, scratching posts and corner protectors in strategically favourable spots, proactive training is of course also going to be useful.

Cats learn quickly on the basis of observation – by observing us humans as well – and a bit of scratching with your fingernails on the new scratching object will quickly attract the cat's attention, above all when it is ritualised into an invitation to play. The use of catnip, too, stimulates the interest of many cats (something like two thirds are susceptible to it, the rest are indifferent), and scratching boards are frequently pretreated with it or include it as an accessory.

Interactive play also gives the opportunity of putting the scratching post at the focus of proceedings, and young cats will learn directly that they can work off their excitement, or for that matter their frustration, right there on the spot.

And last but not least there is the informal *click* in an everyday context, which is your way of telling your cat at any time that it has just done something right! As a result you have brought this form of interaction, which generally takes place in undesirable places, under educational control: the cat scratches at the designated place, and gets rewarded for it – in the form of attention or play. When undesirable scratching occurs, this has arisen by chance and through negligence – with proper education, cats will learn how to attract attention by scratching in the right places.

The challenge is simply to see the cat when it is behaving correctly and react positively to this, rather than waiting till it does something you don't want and then telling it off.

Climbing facilities – the third dimension

Scratching and climbing opportunities are very often combined in a scratching tree as an all-inclusive combined package. But if we want to understand a cat's needs, it can still be helpful to view the different forms of behaviour – climbing, hiding and scratching – separately. It will not always be possible to cover all these needs in the right places with just one scratching tree, however big it is.

Cats live in all three dimensions of space, and use vertical structures like tables, kitchen dressers and shelves without embarrassment as a part of their living space. Above all for indoor cats – and still more so in households with several cats – it is actually indispensable to extend the cat's space by offering access to the second and third levels of the apartment. In this way even a relatively small living environment can be upgraded enormously, and indeed, in small apartments, it may even be essential to make the height of the room accessible as living space for the cat. As a relatively small predator, cats sometimes just feel safer when they can observe what is going on from a secure height, and so retain a certain feeling of control.

With access to the third dimension, even small apartments can be made into a cat-friendly living space..

Apart from the feeling of security, however, it is also the need for social contact, a wanting to be involved, that motivates many cats to jump on the table or dresser. There are lots of interesting things going on there, after all, which a wide-awake active cat would like to take a look at. Friendly gestures of greeting and contact take place between friendly cats through nose contact. But when cats are stuck on the floor, then our legs would be the only contact zone available. Not all cats are fond of being picked up, and crawling on the floor to meet the cat at its own level is a rather eccentric form of greeting when performed by human beings. So what can be more natural for the cat than to look for a more elevated position, where it can actually engage in personal contact, in the place where we are *us* – the face? Just for this reason alone, cats should have at least some places at a height where they can have social contact with humans.

With the positive educational approach described in this book, it is fundamentally possible to declare one or two places to be taboo zones, if it is absolutely necessary – but of course this cannot be guaranteed to work when you are out of the room. This means that if the cat has succeeded in finding exciting smells or tasty crumbs on the kitchen dresser or dining room table just once, this will be enough incentive for it to revisit the place, just on the off chance...

If your idea of education includes a total ban on cats' jumping on furniture – if you want your cat to be exclusively restricted to the floor, or to just a few dedicated scratching objects – you would do well to rethink your project in terms of the needs of the living animal!

Even without a ceiling-high scratching tree, it is perfectly easy to give a cat access to the third dimension – a Cat's Trapeze, cat walks, scratching pillars on the wall or empty spaces on the shelf are simple and cheap solutions for furnishing an apartment in cat-friendly style.

Resting and hiding places

Another basic need not always sufficiently considered – above all in modern open-plan apartments – is a sufficiency of places for hiding and withdrawing into. As well as places where they can sit at a height, cats occasionally look for places of retreat where they are shielded from the gaze. For insecure, stressed or fearful cats, such hiding places are essential – and even grown cats who are good friends spend as much as half of their time out of the sight of their friends.

A fundamental principle for cats is *to see without being seen* – never mind whether they are sitting on the floor or at a height. Cats are real experts at blending in with their background so that they become practically invisible. Sometimes it even looks as if they have a fundamental understanding of the colours and structures of their environment, enabling them to slot into it in the most unobtrusive way.

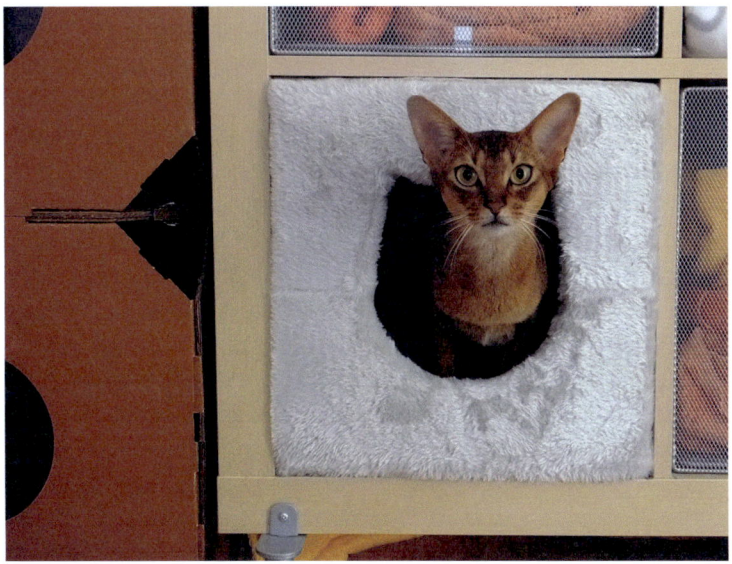

Hiding places and retreats can easily be provided on shelves.

Cats love to be invisible by blending in with the background.

If they are not given appropriate places for withdrawal, cats will often take refuge in the most inaccessible and disgusting corner of the apartment – the furthest corner under the bed, the gap between the fridge and the kitchen wall, the tiny space behind the stereo or the washing machine. What all these places have in common is that they are not really comfortable, so that a cat cannot just feel to some degree safe and out of sight, but can also easily relax. When a new cat – whether it is a kitten or a grown cat – moves in for the first time, these dusty disreputable corners should all be barricaded off and rendered inaccessible if possible. Instead you can offer a variety of small dens and inviting hiding places that are really cat-friendly, and not just desperate last-ditch solutions because the cat can't find any other refuge. The cheapest and simplest solutions are cardboard boxes, which are positioned in such a way that the opening is on the side and not on top. You can pad them out with a soft blanket or a rolled-up towel. Cats are particularly fond of the feeling of leaning on something and having limits –

you could practically say that the smaller the box is that they squeeze into, the better for their purposes.

Far and away the most popular play opportunity and hiding place – Sunnyboy squeezes into a small cardboard box.

Along with the properties of the cat's retreat – softly padded, warm or cool, etc. – the location is also a significant factor. If a cat rejects a new cushion or cosy den it is offered, it may be a case of the material, of the characteristics, the means of access or for that matter of the environment. Three to six weeks are an appropriate interval to vary the place, if a cat shows no interest at all in the den. Personal preferences will hardly be influenced by education, but you can at least familiarise the cat with the place with the help of target exercises and play.

Above all in terms of their feelings about resting places and retreats cats have enormously marked differences, which again will repeatedly change with age, the seasons and the cat's level of development. Here the only course open to you is to improvise, and draw conclusions from the behaviour of your cat.

Simple and space-saving retreats can be made with little hammocks hung under tables or chairs or on radiators; dens can be incorporated in climbing trees or shelves. Tunnels can be easily changed, with different lengths and configurations, and used as hiding places for interactive play.

Hammocks under a chair or coffee table are space-saving options for creating a cat retreat.

The transport box

Far and away the most important possibility of retreat – right from the word go – is offered by the transport box or cat carrier.

A transport box or bag should definitely be a constant feature in the cat's living environment, and what is more, should be its own personal home within the home.

Carriers that sit in the cellar, and only show up when the cat needs to go to the vet, have a negative prospect, just because the cat has not had the chance to get used to them.

The transport box should be an important retreat for the cat, one that it likes and where it feels comfortable and secure.

When the cat has to travel, then at least it will always have its own personal place of security even when it is out of the house.

And even for daily exercises, like the starting box game and periods of quiet learning, as a mobile home or for walks outdoors, the transport box has an exceptionally important function to fulfil.

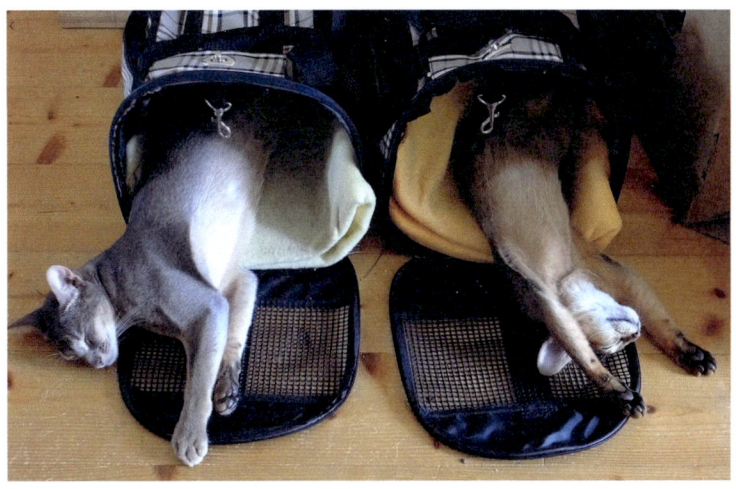

Transport boxes should be an important place of retreat for the cat, and always a part of its living space — Skyboy and Fiji File sleep relaxedly in their transport bags.

If it is really to be adequate in supplying all these functions – and not just for the annual trip to the vet – a transport box needs to meet a number of criteria:
- Not too big, or closely adapted to the size of the cat – remember the cat's preference for small boxes it can squeeze into; and carrying a cat in a smaller box is considerably more comfortable for both parties.
- If you already have bigger boxes, you can pad them out with a thick towel or a blanket; a rolled-up towel or cat bed with a raised surround gives greater stability for car journeys.
- Hygiene – easy to clean.

- Solid plastic boxes which can be taken apart quietly and quickly in just a few actions, without using a set of tools, are ideal.
- The door should be detachable to the front, and have an effective fastening which prevents it from blocking parts of the entrance when it is opened.
- An opening at the top is optional – with a well educated cat, there is no problem getting it into the box, as you can just say *Get in*.
- Safety – you don't want the cat getting out of it when you are on the road.
- Transport bags – these are not quite as secure as boxes, and sometimes lose their shape when the door is opened; but they are generally easier to carry, and in view of their flexibility take up less space.
- For longer trips or stays in the box (e.g. if the box is being used as a sick bay), collapsible dog boxes are a very suitable solution.

Large collapsible boxes are suitable for extended trips in the car, or as a restricted space for occasional quiet learning (or when you have a sick cat in need of R&R).

If you really want to make the transport box function as such an important place for the cat, not only should it be a part of the cat's living space, it should also form part of regular entertaining learning games, and be associated with a certain factor of joyful surprise.

Hiding treats or toys in the box is the simplest technique of passive habituation; and if you occasionally offer a scent of valerian or catnip, that helps make the carrier an exciting place which the cat will like to check out.

In the starting box game, the cat learns to get into the box voluntarily and with positive expectations, and to wait there for an increasing length of time.

In order to establish the box as a place for sleeping and resting, put your young cat into it repeatedly at times when it is evidently tired. Close the door from time to time, so that the cat gets used to it.

> **NB: when it exits the box, there should *always* be something fabulous for the cat – a meal, a game or a treat. But you must take care not to overtax the tolerance of your kitten, so that it gets restless or tries to fight its way out of the box! If you are unlucky enough to have missed the appropriate moment, try somehow to get your cat's attention back, and then open the box when it is has been quiet for a moment.**

Entertainment

Meaningful entertainment is perhaps the most frequently ignored and unrecognised feline need. The general opinion is that cats entertain themselves, and apart from providing food and a toilet you don't have to look after them a great deal, because they can fend for themselves and don't need anything added. This may be true up to a certain degree if the cat has friends and the opportunity of roaming and hunting, when it can come and go as it likes by way of the cat door and, taken all in all, lives alongside its humans rather than with them.

But once a cat's living conditions have changed so radically that it no longer has any influence in these quarters, its entertainment needs rise, and so does the responsibility of its owner.

And indeed it is often the creative solutions that active cats think up, when they try to create a little more entertainment in the monotony of everyday, which lead to many problems in the human-feline relationship. Even relations between cats are not immune from going downhill, if one of them has to serve as one-sided entertainment for the other.

Cats are often thought to be *well-behaved* when they just do their job as an emotional partner for their persons, inconspicuously and without making demands. But the deal is often somewhat unbalanced – to the detriment of the happily active cat, who needs more than just a few petting sessions (which are actually more to our benefit), a fur mouse on the carpet and a few extra scooby treats.

Autonomous entertainment

Fortunately cats are indeed capable of occupying themselves very well, up to a certain point – they do not on any account need an ongoing entertainment programme! Quite on the contrary – it is actually very sensible to give the cat opportunities of autonomous activity.

For young cats it is automatic to embark on hunting games with all kinds of small objects – they will practise without interruption hunting strategies like lying in ambush, creeping up on a thing and pouncing on imaginary prey. This kind of independent game however becomes less common – more or less, depending on the cat's personality – with experience and adulthood. The great majority of adult cats, according to their owners, have ceased to play – listless lying around is simply thought to be normal cat behaviour. But this only applies when you take the independent boisterous playfulness of the young cat as a reference point!

Your average adult cat is much easier to motivate with meaningful activities crucial to life – a dusty mouse toy that has been lying around for months is unlikely to be seen as a genuine prey.

With the best of intentions, we deprive our cats of one of the most genuinely meaningful patterns of behaviour by handing them their food on a plate without any expenditure of physical or mental effort on their part! So all the strategies discussed in the section on feeding are the most natural way of giving a cat opportunities of autonomous occupation.

But besides this there are other possibilities of channelling the entertainment needs of a kitten in an acceptable direction at an early stage, without your being expected to turn into a permanent entertainer for your cat.

- Things to play with and carry around: an alternating variety of small prey substitutes like stuffed mice, balls, valerian bags and so on are suitable for autonomous hunting games and can be carried around; little collection boxes give the cat later the opportunity of itself fetching the toy it wants to play with.
- Things that are prone to move: balls that can be pushed along tracks, objects mounted on the wall with an elastic wire.
- Things with an odour: many cat toys are already prepared with scents to make them more attractive. Catnip and valerian are the most common. Also feathers and natural materials from outdoors.
- Things to destroy: a roll of toilet paper or kitchen roll is cheap, and can be shredded into confetti without doing great damage, but it provides a great deal of entertainment; cats also like puncturing and shredding cardboard boxes and paper with their teeth.
- Things to throw down: as talented experimenters, cats like to observe the force of gravity – and they are fascinated by watching small objects and pushing them with their paw till

they drop. As it is hopeless to wean them from this fascination, the best plan is to give them approved places from the start, where they can go on legally putting the force of gravity to the test.

Toilet paper and kitchen rolls are a cheap entertainment programme for active young cats.

- Things to chew: cats who like chewing, above all during the change of teeth, will gnaw on corners, edges or any other projecting objects. With the help of a stable clip you can fix stiff leather bits, paper sticks, drinking straws, dried meat or hard chews (dog chews) in places where your cat can get at them.

- Things to explore: cats are inquisitive, and to keep their interest alive, the important thing is to offer them something new from time to time. Biodegradable starch chips from packaging, cardboard boxes, paper bags with removed or cut through handles, a large egg, feathers you happen upon, fir cones, stones, various insects... There are countless possibilities of making a cat's life more exciting by introducing novelties of all kinds.

All sorts of new things to investigate –
Skyboy and Fiji File have been given a big nandu egg to sniff at.

- Water games: there are cats with a pronounced predilection for water, who will like splashing around with drinking fountains, water bowls or other containers. Water basins can be provided either on the balcony, or as a basin inside a larger basin, in order to save the floors and other surroundings from floods. Ice cubes too, or ice balls made from water bomb air balloons, will give some cats many happy hours of summer entertainment.

Technological toys

Modern entertainment electronics has not stopped short of cats, creating further possibilities of autonomous activity. These include technological mice, hexbugs and birds that produce chirping sounds – some battery-powered ones can propel themselves around independently.

Hexbugs are microrobots that mimic insects. They are designed with children in mind, but cats will also be fascinated. Different places of use, like the bath tub or a plastic box, will make the game still more entertaining when you throw in the small electronic cockroach. At the same time cats will get used to experiencing the vibrations in a playful situation, so that the noise and vibration of the vet's clipper will no longer make such a threatening impact.

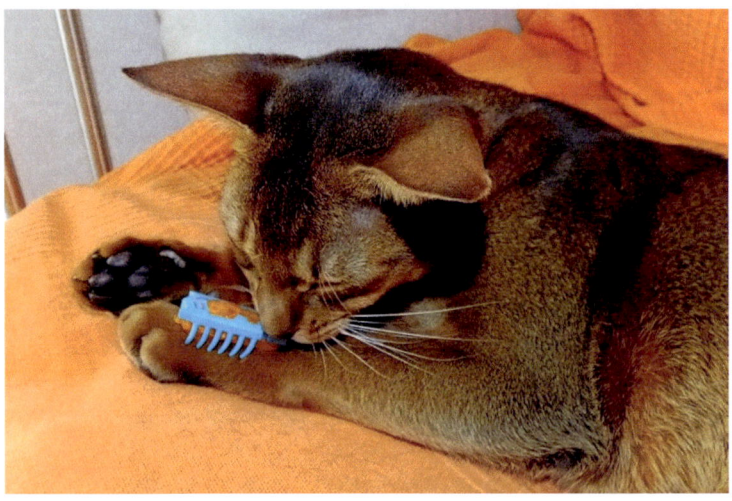

Playing with one of his favourite toys, aka the Cockroach, Fiji File at the same time gets used to feeling vibrations on his own body.

A similar gadget is the Shru – this egg-shaped cat toy moves autonomously in unpredictable ways while producing beeping sounds. A USB interface makes it possible to analyse the cat's play, and based on this develops new and individual rhythms.

Tablets as well now offer numerous apps which simulate the movement of prey – though only in two-dimensional form. As with laser pointers, there are cats who can get somewhat obsessed with this kind of game. Others will soon get bored with the fruitless chase, or they try to get at the mice, beetles or flies that are buzzing around underneath the Tablet, or by biting into it.

All these electronic games can certainly be amusing for some cats, but still they are not a substitute – at best they can only be a supplement – for interactive play with a human being.

Modern technocats: Fiji File and Windy Whisper play with a mouse on the Tablet.

Exercise

Although cats are not notable as running animals, some feline types nonetheless are very given to exercise. Even when extended into the third dimension, human dwellings are still very small living spaces for a cat, and do not offer a wide range of exercise opportunities. One autonomous possibility of encouraging exercise is a running wheel. These are similar to the wheels you use with hamsters and mice who are kept in cages – just a few sizes bigger. Although in view of their size they do take up a certain amount of space, they are of enormous benefit in increasing the cat's exercise options – they are suitable for channelling both leisurely strolling, and boisterous attacks of frantic activity. Cats who are used to the running wheel learn very quickly how to work off their superfluous energy, and sometimes also their frustration or tension, by converting it into movement.

> NB: with any kind of facilities for encouraging autonomous activity, you absolutely must be aware of all the safety aspects – string, rubber bands, small parts that can be swallowed and so on are not suitable for an unsupervised autonomous feline entertainment programme.

With the help of a cat running wheel, even indoor cats can meet their exercise needs – Windy Whisper and Fiji File having a short sprint.

Interactive entertainment

However well cats can cope, for a certain time, with being left on their own – focusing on personal cat matters like grooming, observing, resting, sleeping and of course getting their food – cats as pets are still not totally without expectations.

One of the cat's most important activities in real life would be hunting – and this is indeed what cats do best. Not all cats – and here there are considerable differences, probably also based on genetic predisposition – have an equally pronounced passion for hunting. Cats with a relatively low hunting motivation are pleasant companions, and you can share a house with them without any problem, even if you only spend the occasional evening playing with them. But really ambitious hunter cats, above all in their youth, are positively exhausting – verging on impossible – to keep in a small apartment. When there is no prey available, they will direct their hunting activities to anything moving – feet, hands, even heads, dogs, small children and other cats will not be immune to sudden ambush from behind. For this kind of cat above all it is exceptionally important to teach them consistently, right from the start, what they can best do with their hunting energy!

Interactive hunting games

Interactive hunting games are an important educational element for all cats, because they channel the activity of the cat in a meaningful way and are pure life quality. For a cat that is free to roam and can have its own hunting experiences outdoors these interactive games are not so important, but they are still very useful as a reward and as part of education in self-control. An important condition here is that these hunting activities should be made really irresistible. And here it is more up to us humans to learn something – since cats already know all about play hunting!

What to play with?

Prey that the cat finds interesting will as a rule be much smaller than the cat itself – the cat's proverbial typical prey is the mouse; and then of course there are also all kinds of other small creatures, from butterflies to birds, from worms to snakes and lizards, from bugs to bats. Not all these kinds of prey will end up being eaten – cats are often more concerned with hunting for its own sake, with catching something.

A first step for a successful hunting game with your cat is to find out whether it has individual preferences for a specific kind of prey, or is basically an all-rounder who is happy to hunt anything that looks like prey.

Skyboy carrying his toy prey to a new play area

The basic categories of prey are the following:
- Small mammals like mice, shrews, rats etc.
- Flying and crawling insects like butterflies, dragonflies, flies, spiders, beetles etc.
- Birds
- Crawling animals like lizards, snakes, worms etc.
- Fishes, sometimes also frogs.

Just as kittens learn from their mother's bringing prey to them what is good to eat, at the same time they develop a preference for this type of prey, which in some circumstances they may stay with very consistently. With cats who have grown up in the home, these preferences are directed not to real live prey but to certain toys with which they have grown up. Find out what your kitten's favourite toy is, before you take it home with you!

Educating a cat also involves makes this familiar spectrum of toy prey more flexible by adding new experiences and so extending it.

Commercial cat's toys are very often too big, not to say monstrous, even for an adult cat. Along with the small size – you can take a butterfly or small mouse as a reference point – noises (soft rustling and crackling, possibly squeaking) and the feel of the texture in the mouth (natural materials like feathers, fur, leather or soft textiles) are also important aspects of the cat's prey. The colour, on the other hand, is less important – many so-called cat's toys are really very much more like garish children's toys than cat-friendly prey substitutes. Two colour strategies seem to have particular interest for cats – either sharply contrasting with the background or well camouflaged, so as to be principally detectable by movement. For an irresistible toy prey, it would make more sense to follow the example of fly fishermen, who expend a great deal of effort to create a lure that is as true to nature as possible, in preference to harshly coloured children's toys.

Laser pointers might help in the short term for warming up purposes, as a highly intensive stimulus for feline activity, but as a cat's toy in isolation they are unsuitable. The extraordinary intensity of the light stimulus combined with emptiness rapidly leads to frustration, because there is no real prey to be caught – however, many cats do develop a compulsive attachment to playing with the laser pointer. Besides, the object of interactive play is not to wind up the cat till it is panting for breath for the amusement of children or visitors…

All good prey objects are subject to the rule that they must be moved and controlled by a human, at sufficient distance from the cat. So anything attached to a stick, elastic wire, string or fishing rod is highly suitable. The distance is a measure of personal safety, as in play hunting a certain measure of roughness is allowed; and then too, it respects the personal space of the cat – if you were too close it would spoil the feeling of the game.

So you should look for a fine assortment of cat's toys, which you can change regularly, at least in a weekly rhythm. As we are concerned with prey objects which are designed to give the cat a realistic feeling of the hunt, toys are basically to be seen as consumables and not as a one-off purchase. And of course there is no reason why you shouldn't make prey toys yourself out of the simplest materials – strictly speaking, just a simple piece of parcel string will suffice.

Although it seems a practical solution and they are of course always available for the purpose, fingers are *not* to be used as prey for cats! Especially not for kittens, who have not yet fully learned how to control themselves. If you extend your fingers or hands as prey, you are giving your kitten an open invitation to slaughter them…

NB: interactive prey toys should only be got out during play sessions, and should not be available to the cat at all times!

When to play?

As hunters, cats are above all active in the twilight period – the early hours of morning or evening are thus a natural activity phase for them, when it is particularly easy to get them interested in a hunting game. But during the day as well most cats have the occasional short active phase, alternating with longer periods of rest.

Around feeding time – either before or after – is also a good time for playing, as it answers to a cat-specific activity phase.

The important thing, anyway, is to stick to these play times with something approaching regularity – then they become an eagerly awaited fixed point on the day's agenda, and the cat will remain actively involved, even into old age.

How to play?

The most important principle for an interactive hunting game with the cat is that a realistic prey wants to survive! This means you get your mock prey to behave in such a way that it cautiously but heedlessly darts from one hiding place to the next, and tries to survive the evening. One of the reasons why adult cats, above all, lose interest in playing is the way in which they are harassed, sometimes practically menaced by these toy preys. No natural prey would be so impatient in demanding won't you please, please just get on with it and finally catch me…

Another reason for dissatisfaction with the cat's hunting game is that their humans start to get restive – because it seems nothing is happening. The cat just sits there and looks, and looks and looks… This has to do with the misunderstanding that interactive hunting play only occurs when the cat actually tries to catch its prey. But for the cat the excitement of the game starts long before that – when it selects its potential prey, observes, plans, changes position and perhaps goes over the spring it is going to make several times in its head. This incorrect attitude of expectation – the cat is playing when it runs after its prey – only applies in the case of very young cats. The older your cat gets, the more realistically you must organise these games. When young cats have practised hunting often enough in play, they know how to do it. Adult cats hunt calmly, patiently and with maximum efficiency! This is admittedly rather boring for human beings – but interactive hunting play is not principally intended as entertainment for humans. If, on the other hand, we start to observe the hunting style and expressive behaviour of the cat, it can actually be quite entertaining.

In order to set up a hunting situation as realistically as possible, it is important that both the prey and the cat should have sufficient cover for hiding and stalking. Spectacular hunting springs can above all be launched when the prey disappears out of the cat's vision, or dashes quite fast from one hiding place to the next. When a cat has caught its prey, the latter may either play dead or make efforts to escape – both are part of an exciting hunting sequence, and playful cats be quite good at conveying what continuation of the game they favour.

Cats are moreover solitary hunters, and in a household with several cats it is practically always necessary to give the cats exclusive play sessions separately from one another. It is almost always the case that one of the cats is more quickly resolved, braver and quicker to spring, so that the slower, more reflectively hunting cat experiences more frustration than pleasure in the game. Adult cats do also respect the personal space and prey of another cat, but having to attend all the time to the prey while simultaneously observing the position of the other cat can be rather stressful for some cats. In order to get these more cautious cats out of their inhibitions and encourage them to play with greater abandon, the more impulsive cat, after its first play, can be put in the box for a break. Finally it can be given another short play session as a reward for waiting in the box. As an alternative, you can of course also play with two cats at once if they each have a toy, and the game is organised in such a way that there is some distance between them so they do not get in each other's way.

Here's a summary overview of points relating to interactive hunting play:
- Plan fairly regular play times – ideally in the evening.
- Play alone – cats are solitary hunters.
- Sufficient cover and hiding places needed, for prey and hunters.
- Change the toy at least once a week – every cat has its own preferences.
- Interactive hunting games are above all for the cat, not for the human.
- Realistic prey wants to survive, not to be caught.
- Fingers are not to be used as prey.

Social play

In their living together, many human-feline relationships develop a very personal form of social play. These may be catching or hiding games, scaring each other mutually or various forms of play fights. Young tom cats above all can get very rough in this situation, when they claw onto your hands, lower arm or feet with their front paws, bite and kick with their hind legs. Even the smallest suggestion of this fighting behaviour (which generally also has a sexual undertone) should be consistently channelled with the help of stuffed animals, play cushions or scratching and biting rolls, ideally scented with valerian, as educational helpers. If a young macho tom has once got into uninhibited fighting mode with his ears laid back, every one of your movements will just be an invitation to greater brutality – as a precaution, you should immediately offer him his wrestling partner, holding it between his paws and against his stomach. Although it may appear tempting, punishments in this situation are not really appropriate, as either they result in even tougher fighting efforts on the cat's part or else the emotion switches into fear, and the game becomes defence in earnest.

> NB: these inanimate sparring partners for educational purposes need to be close to the cat's own size, but should on no account be frightening.

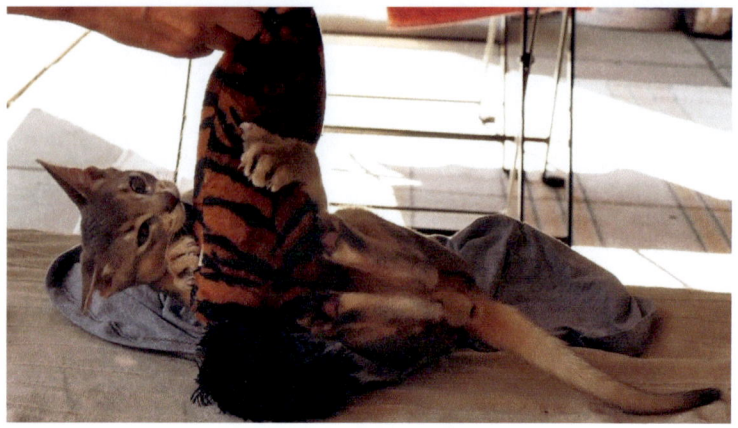

Sunnyboy fights with his wrestling partner – a useful helper in his education as the hands are spared!

Safety

Along with lifestyle elements that are important to cats, safety in the house and garden is an important factor in relation to education in an extended sense. Taboo zones and prohibitions can create a kind of safety, but as a foundation for a safe cat's life they definitely fall short. This is above all because active prohibitions only teach most cats one quite essential lesson: they are only going to do it in future when there are no humans present to tell them off – a very logical conclusion and from the point of view of the cat, a sensible learning process! It follows that passive safety measures make much better sense, and are more effective. These can start from the point where you try to picture what dangers a cat like this – and especially a kitten – may be exposed to.

The worry that cats may burn their paws on the **hot plates of the stove** is high on the list of reasons why cats should not be allowed in the kitchen or on the working surface. Although this fear is not entirely unjustified, the consequences for a cat are actually less serious and dangerous than is the case with many other potential accidents. In the worst case scenario the cat will get a few blisters on its paws, along with the abiding life lesson that it had better either avoid this place in future, or else be a great deal more cautious.

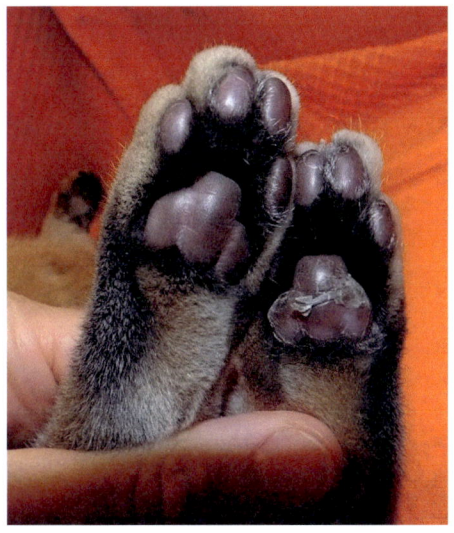

Just a slight burn on the paw pads, but an enduring lesson for life.

High up on the list of factors causing accidents to cats – and sad to say, death in many cases – are quite simple things like windows and doors.

Hopper windows can be a death trap for cats, because the gap at the bottom closes so tightly that once they have slipped into it they can hardly get out again, and just become more tightly wedged. Depending on whether the cat is left hanging by the chest or the pelvis, it can only look forward to a more or less long, but in any case very painfully drawn out death. Cats who are caught by the pelvis may in exceptional cases be saved if they are discovered soon enough, but they are often paralysed for a long time.

> **Essential precaution: don't leave windows on the tilt at all, or protect windows of this kind with a screen or wedges.**

Falls from the window or from the balcony are another real danger for cats – it is not a question whether they are going to fall, only of when. This applies even to cats who have spent their whole lives balancing on a balcony railing on the sixth floor. An insect flying past or a bird will make a youthful cat with a liking for the hunt forget that it can fly only to a limited degree, and it will lose its balance. And older or overweight cats have often already lost something of their youthful elegance. Accidents are particularly likely to occur in spring, on the first sunny days – the door to the room with the open windows may be closed, but the cat only needs a brief moment to slip into the room, spring up onto the window ledge and then… with no hesitation, plunge into the abyss.

> **Essential precaution: protective nets or screens for windows and the balcony.**

Falls can also occur in the house of course, when kittens fall through open stairwells or galleries or from very high scratching trees, cupboards or shelves. Young cats are particularly susceptible to such accidents when they are playing and rampaging around. Fortunately many of these falls will be without serious consequences, above all when the cat is young and quite light – because it is also elastic and very mobile. And with increasing experience and age, the risk of such accidents is reduced.

More critical are falls where the cat does not fall on its own, but at the same time knocks over furniture or pulls down heavy objects that land on it. Similarly to situations with small children who pull themselves up on things, in cat households articles of furniture like this should be secured or fixed to the wall. Even smaller objects like ironing boards or laundry racks can in the worst case scenario prove fatal to a kitten. Particularly enticing features are hanging ribbons or loose ends, which encourage the cat to jump up or climb.

Essential precaution: fasten securely or stow away potentially dangerous objects; temporarily cordon off critical areas with a screen or netting.

The household harbours many potential dangers – even a falling laundry rack can be fatal to kittens.

Getting wedged in something can also have fatal consequences, particularly for small kittens – typical danger points are the folding mechanisms of sofas and foldaway beds, and doors that slam. The impulse to close the door as quickly as possible before the cat gets out all too often results in trapped paws or tails. Similar accidents happen with draughts, because cats like to linger indecisively between the door and the hinge, where they then get trapped by the slamming door.

> **Essential precaution: door stops, and mindfulness.** Cats are extremely quick, and generally it is better either to hold them tight at once as a precaution or to call them back, rather than racing to close the door.

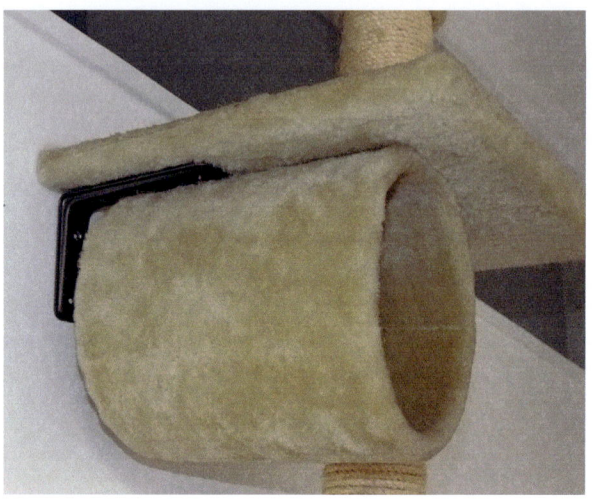

Scratching frames and shelves need to be secured against toppling over in cat households.

Ribbons, strings and rubber bands present irresistible attractions, and a kitten can make practically anything like this into a game. All kinds of attached string harbour a certain risk of strangulation, especially long rubber bands such as are used in cat's toys. Another problem is the potential damage a cat can cause when it chews through strings, e.g. those of blinds or shutters. All kinds of thread-shaped objects – from embroidery silk to wool, from gift wrap ribbon to parcel string – when eaten can result in potentially life-threatening intestinal obstruction. Cats do not even have to decide for themselves to eat a string of this kind – sometimes it seems to them that there is no alternative to swallowing the thread, because the hooks on their tongue make it impossible to spit it out.

> **Essential precaution: keep safe or safely stowed away; critical cat's toys should be used only interactively and under supervision.**

For some cats, **electric cords of all kinds** are no less interesting than thread. They offer a certain resistance to chewing, and the plastic coating seems eminently suitable for trying out the kitten's just emerging little teeth. Apart from the not inconsiderable damage this can cause, electrical cables are of course extremely dangerous.

> **Essential precaution: cable guards or wraps with aluminium foil, keep safe and offer cats who like chewing sufficient alternative options to try their teeth on.**

Improbable as it may seem, the **washing machine** can actually be a death trap for cats. Load it up with laundry and leave it open for a while before starting it, and not a few cats have been known to elect this little cave as a place to snooze in...

> **Essential precaution: close the washing machine, and check it before switching on.**

There are numerous **small objects** which may be eaten by cats and which can cause an intestinal obstruction. This includes principally anything that smells of food in some way – like sausage clips or olive stones, plastic wrappings, leather, coins, Lego pieces, and for that matter cat's toys which have been chewed and eaten. Various foam and synthetic materials, like rubber rings, are particularly attractive to some cats. On the one hand they often contain softening agents, and on the other they offer a chewing resistance which cats clearly find exciting.

> Essential precaution: potential foreign bodies should be kept safe, and if your cat is addicted to synthetics, you had better avoid rubber toys.

Toxic house plants will be chewed by cats for preference when they have no access to suitable grass. In case of nausea cats have an irresistible urge to eat fibrous structures like grass, often because it functions as an emetic. If a cat cannot find grass, it will choose another substance that seems to it suitable – indoor plants, even if they have round or thick leaves, dried flowers, hay, and even textile materials like a woollen jumper or a towel. It can happen that the cat's very first experience of nausea, and the material it then resorts to, has a determining influence on its later decisions in the same situation.

For kittens, plants of all kinds are interesting not just for nibbling and teasing apart, they are also a wonderful playground: rolling in a plant, snatching at leaves and flowers, bending stems or climbing up on them are all quite normal modes of behaviour for a young cat.

> Essential precaution: donate toxic plants to a household without cats, or keep them in a place where no cat can possibly get at them. Valuable plants should be protected, or kept safe as a temporary measure. Always ensure that the cat has access to a suitable cat grass in different varieties.

Other toxic substances are ingested by cats only on rare occasions – with one important exception: antifreeze mixtures containing glycol.

Access to the outdoors

The possibility of roaming freely is of course an important factor for the cat's quality of life – even if it is not always without risk.

Thus it turns out that not all living conditions support access to the outdoors in a form that is relatively hazard-free, while on the other hand not all cats can be kept exclusively indoors. This is another thing you need to think about early on when choosing a kitten.

The possibility of roaming naturally has implications in various respects for the cat's education. Cats who from early youth have been able to come and go by way of a cat door will have a much less dependent relationship with their humans than pure indoor cats. The intensity of the cat's education will be less, just in view of its independence – the cat will live just as cats always have lived.

The more restricted the cat's possibilities of adventure, on the other hand, the more essential is a thoroughgoing education – because it becomes, directly or indirectly, the essential factor for the life quality of the cat.

Depending on the neighbourhood and the traffic on the roads, there are countless different ways of letting cats live outdoors, with different spatial and temporal boundaries.

The version with minimal control – unlimited freedom in terms of time and space – means that the cat can come and go through the cat door just as it likes.

As free-ranging cats should definitely be labelled with a microchip, a cat flap with chip control is also a very sensible investment. It not only prevents strange cats – who of course are also familiar with the principle of the cat flap – from intruding into your home, where they may terrorise your cat in its own private environment, it also supports a variety of programme settings to determine when and in what direction your cat is allowed to go.

Controlled forms of roaming are restricted in terms of either time or space or both, and so increasingly reduce the associated risk. Road accidents are among the commonest causes of cat deaths, and unfortunately cats are not altogether safe even in zones with traffic calming.

Absolutely no roaming at night, as a time limit, is a good approach if you want to reduce risk, and quite feasible with the help of technical solutions the cat door offers.

Far and away the safest alternative to unlimited roaming is the spatial restriction of a cat-proof fenced-in garden, the structure of which is such as to allow the cat plenty of opportunity for adventure. This solution is a contemporary and modern form of keeping a cat, not just in areas with a lot of traffic, but also and in particular in densely populated districts with small gardens (also bearing in mind that the neighbours may not be too fond of cats).

There are various technical solutions here, ranging from the simple and cheap electric fence (similar to that used with chickens, sheep, cows or horses) to wire netting, and then there are expensive and elaborate fence systems involving a smooth surface or an overhang.

A cat who has not yet become acquainted with the big wide world beyond the fence will be much more ready to put up with this limitation of its experiential space – so you should decide at an early stage which solution you are inclined to consider. Cats are moreover extremely lively escape artists, and well capable of using their planning abilities to observe you in the process of construction, and subsequently discover all the gaps and weak points in the miniature Alcatraz of your garden.

Just as in an indoor setting, so too in the garden a cat-friendly environmental structure which makes it easy for the cat to be *well-behaved* is a fundamental component of education.

Here are some of the resources which make a cat's garden attractive:

- Water – just a small water basin will increase the attractiveness of the garden, not just for cats, but also for many small animals which cats find interesting.
- Resting and hiding places in the shade and the sun, for observation purposes – *to see, without being seen.*
- Stones or piles of stones which store heat, and also offer small caves as hiding places for animals.
- Scented plants – from catnip to valerian and all herbs.
- Flowering plants which attract butterflies and other insects.
- Clumps of grass – for eating, playing or flattening.

- Outdoor toilet – above all in small gardens and households with more than one cat it may be important to offer a roofed outdoor toilet, which can be cleaned out when necessary.
- Interactive play in the garden – prey dummies are twice as interesting in the garden at the twilight hour.

Taken all in all, the cat-friendly garden gives the feeling of a small wilderness, in every way opposed to the sterile manicured lawn!

A screened off window balcony offers protection along with views, and can become a valuable living space for the cat.

The size is not such an important factor for the cat – just a few square metres of wilderness, or untended garden area, have a whole lot more to offer as an adventure playground than a gigantic garden that is painstakingly mown once a week. Even if you do not want to make any cat-proof boundary around your garden, this increases the chances that the cat will stay in your garden because there is enough there for it to experience.

The minimal version of outdoor access for the cat is a balcony or terrace, which like an indoor environment or garden can be designed to yield a valuable living space for the cat just with the help of a few small structural elements. Securing the area with a screen or netting is one of the obligatory measures in such a case, and there is no way of getting around it!

Before a young cat is allowed out into the garden, it needs to have learned a few things. These include of course its name, and the signal *Come*, or coming when you whistle. It should also have already mastered the exercise of responding to your call when it is shut in – *Kitty-kat, say meow!* – before the cat is allowed out on its own.

If you want to give your cat unlimited roaming privileges – without a secured garden, that is to say – you would be well advised only to let it out alone and unaccompanied after it reaches the age of puberty. If you allow a young cat to roam independently and without control from a very early stage – from the eighth or twelfth week of life – there is a very high risk that it will make itself independent and develop an opportunistic life alongside its human family. At the same time it still has a lot to learn in terms of life experience, and the dangers outdoors are many. Around puberty is also the typical age for castration, so that you won't have either unwanted kitten, or your cat going missing for days at a time when driven by its hormones.

With very young cats, around the age of eight to twelve weeks, shared excursions into the garden are a very good opportunity of gradually showing them the big wide world, without losing your connection. The older the cat is, the wider in the nature of things becomes its radius, so that from the twelfth to sixteenth week of life it might be advisable to try excursions with harness and a leash. The best thing is when you start these garden outings with a hungry kitten, and have an attractive new toy with you, so as to have useful motivation ready when you need it.

Whenever you want to call the cat back or take it indoors again, you inform it, like *come home*, and offer it an exceptional treat or even an entire meal. In the first months of being outdoors the time should be limited, and the kitten should be contacted on a regular basis – by calling it, making eye contact, petting or playing. And just to have something to set against the exciting outdoor adventure, so your cat will not be disillusioned when called back to be confined to quarters, little surprises are a help – in the form of treats, or invitations to play with new and untested toys.

From puberty on and as young adults, most cats have a good connection with their humans and above all get used to human life rhythms. The development of these habits makes it a lot easier to establish certain safety rules when the cat goes out – though unfortunately there is no absolute guarantee that with increasing age the cat may not become independent and aloof notwithstanding.

Excursions with or without the leash

Many cats live exclusively indoors – and their numbers go on increasing. And although there are cats who seem quite contented with this arrangement, some of us remain with an uneasy conscience because we feel we are depriving them of something. Sophia Yin, a very remarkable and influential veterinary behaviour specialist, has said: *Cats are the new improved dogs. You can take them for walks, but you don't have to.*

Taking cats for walks is quite different from what it is like with dogs – and frequently involves less walking than standing or sitting! Outdoor excursions with cats are times for sniffing around and observing, rather than covering immense distances in order to get fit. And yet cats are sometimes prepared to accompany you on walks – for instance, if you go for a shared walk with a dog-friend, or else in a safe environment with other human beings.

For indoor cats, outdoor excursions are more adventures and an enrichment of the everyday routine than they are sport. An essential condition is that the cat should actually enjoy it!

For cats with a fearful nature, who in spite of intensive socialisation in the first months start to show signs of fear in puberty, such outings represent stress rather than an interesting experience.

You can take cats for walks – but you don't have to! Sunnyboy not only learned to go for walks on the leash, he also resorted to eye contact when he needed information.

But when you start them early and plan the operation well, many cats will get fun out of these excursions:
- Make sure they are well used to the harness and leash – the cat must let itself be *dressed (let's dress)* without effort, and should think wearing a harness and leash is perfectly normal.
- Every excursion absolutely must start with *Get in*, with the cat's getting into its transport box – however near it is, even if you are just going into the inner court or communal garden –

the cat must *never* cross the threshold of the door on its own and unaided.
- This diversion by way of the transport box brings numerous advantages – the cat learns a sensible ritual for going out, will not sit by the door and beg to go out at inconvenient times and will not be trying at the least opportunity to disappear by the route it is now familiar with.
- When you are outside you will always have the box on hand as a safe place when actual dangers (like strange dogs) threaten, or the cat wants to hide.
- Be inwardly prepared for standing around and waiting – cats are not just small dogs, and they can sit for minutes on the spot just to observe the environment, listen or sniff at every single grass blade and stone.
- Sudden jumps and sprints – after a long phase of sitting around, many cats will launch into a sudden sprint and race away. Stay alert and observe your cat's body language, which gives you warning of this kind of quick start.
- No pulling on the leash. Don't pull on the leash – it is better to entice the cat, who will follow the nose target, a toy or in your footsteps. If you want to shift your ground and the cat doesn't follow, you had better pick it up and carry it.
- Quiet times in the evening or early morning, at the weekend or at night, are most suitable for excursions.
- Choose quiet spots that offer exciting entertainment – for a cat, this could be anything from the radiator of a car to a manhole cover. Excursions in nature, in a meadow, on the edge of a wood or by a stream, can be an excellent idea for a cat who has some experience of these outings. When you actually meet other animals, like chickens, sheep, cows or horses, that increases the adventure factor.
- Caution is advised, in view of all the possibilities of the cat's making a quick exit – cats like to find little openings to slip through in fences, walls and the like, and you won't be able to follow them.
- Cat excursions don't have to take very long – 15 to 30

minutes are often quite enough to satisfy the cat's need of excitement.

On outdoor excursions, Fiji File and Windy Whisper can always resort to the transport bag as a safe place of retreat.

Basic kit – what do cats need?

Before you adopt your kitten, in addition to suitable cat food you need to have the following basic equipment to hand in the home:
- a transport box
- a feeding bowl for moist food
- two or more activity feeding toys for dry food – stationary and mobile
- two litter boxes – of sufficient size, and open
- fine-grained, clumping litter
- two water sources – standing water and water in motion
- two or more scratching objects
- four or more prey toys for interactive games
- a fine and a coarse comb for long-haired cats
- harness and leash
- time and attention.

Development

Kittens develop at headlong speed – in just a few weeks they have matured from the helpless baby into the independent young cat who moves in with us. At about six months they reach puberty, and could actually already have offspring, even if they are themselves not yet quite fully grown. At one to one and a half years most cats have attained to their full physical growth, but they will only be socially mature at the age of three or four years. These developmental changes will of course also be reflected in the different phases of the cat's education.

The first eight weeks are the most sensitive phase, marked by the most intensive learning – this is when the points are set for the rest of the cat's life. When you acquire your kitten, you cannot do anything to change what has happened to date, but the coming months are still a notable learning period, even if a degree slower.

In the months up to around half a year young cats are exceptionally active, and meet new experiences for the most part without any problem. They are easily frightened, but recover with equal rapidity – above all when something that is fun is involved, like a play or a treat. Their concentration is not very well developed as yet – after three or four repetitions of an exercise they are often distracted again, and turn to more exciting things.

Up to puberty, the cat's little brain has already formed countless new links on a daily basis, it has learned a whole lot and integrated its experience with everyday life. And yet it is just at this time that you may have the impression that all the effort of teaching has yielded absolutely no result.

Exercises it has learned already may be quite simply declined – when you invite your young cat into the wish box because it wants something, it just stays standing alongside and behaves as if it has never heard of this exercise. Or you offer a nose target, and the cat just looks at it, then turns away and rejects it. It really does look as if the prejudiced view that cats are ineducable might turn out to be true after all. But this phase does not last long, and it won't help to apply pressure or to practise even more – it is simply going to pass. It seems that this phase of rejection is simply a natural part of the cat's growing up, and it hasn't forgotten anything of what it has learned – quite the reverse!

Youthful tom cats in particular can lose their self-control during puberty, and when playing can get extremely wild and rough. Their physical capacities will improve when the lanky awkwardness of the four to five month old cat develops into more balanced proportions and a better musculature.

As it reaches adulthood, the cat can become increasingly cautious, more restrained, even in some cases fearful. Crucial for the education however is the question what the cat does after its first reaction of panic or retreat – in the best case scenario it will be capable of analysing the situation, based on previous experience and possibly by consulting its human mentor, rather than freezing in terrified paralysis, or losing its head and running away without checking to see if any real danger is involved.

Although the basic character of the cat does not really change, some patterns of behaviour just become more adult. This may in some circumstances mean that physical contact, like petting or cuddling, will not always meet with such an enthusiastic response at all times as it does with kittens. Whereas kittens are very happy to cuddle up to you and seek physical contact, it may be that a grown cat will prefer to sleep alone. Even cats who have grown up together and are good friends start wanting at this age to keep some distance between them at times. Their play habits change – the grown cat is more ambitious, serious and at the same time more effective in its hunting game sequences.

The first step – learning to learn

How cats learn – the theory

In order to put something across to a cat, there needs first of all to be a tiny basis of common language, the lowest common denominator of communication – but human words here are not really a help, at least in the initial phases. *No, Get down, Come* or *Leave it* does not have any great meaning for the cat.

Cats learn – as we all do, incidentally – very effectively from success, occasionally supported by the experience of a failure. Try something out – experience joyful consequences – try it out more frequently, to see if it has the same satisfactory result – and store away the information that this works.

So the first step for a common language of learning is deliberately to put such happy consequences in the cat's path rather than leaving them to chance, where they are incapable of having educational effect – at any rate, an educational effect that you have planned for in advance.

The time window in which the cat can create an unambiguous connection between its experiment, its action, and the positive consequence ensuing, and so learn from it, is quite short. For everyday educational purposes, though, you can pragmatically assume that it comes to one second. Everything that follows an action within one second is associated with it – from the cat's point of view, the one thing determines the other.

Seeing that in an everyday educational context there are things we want to communicate to a cat as a fortunate and desirable success, but these things are not always going to be to hand this very second, there is a practical tool for getting over this hurdle: clicker training.

> Scientific learning theory has developed this immensely versatile tool of clicker training with the aim of marking more complex actions as *successful* (or pinpointing them exactly in terms of time, even over a greater distance), even when at this precise moment you don't have a reward to hand. The origins of clicker training, incidentally, go back to an interesting question: *How do I say to a dolphin that he should cooperate with me and will get something out of it if he jumps through the hoop?* As with cats, you can't really compel a dolphin to do something – you can't just propel him through the air and push him through the hoop in hope that he will learn from this to do it repeatedly of his own accord.

Clicker training is the invisible communication tool with which you can first of all give the cat a *symbolic reward* – this promises the *real reward* which can then be expected to follow. The acoustical success signal of the *click* can be used with great timing precision, and lets the cat know, just like a snapshot, which of its actions has just proved so successful.

This makes it a synthetic, and extremely simple, new level of communication which can be set up between two species who do not speak the same language – dolphins and human beings, or indeed cats and human beings.

This rerouting by way of symbolic reward to real reward is actually only important because and in cases where the time window mentioned earlier between the cat's action and the success achieved is longer than a second.

> Two examples:
> Your kitten sits down, and you give it a small piece of food from your hand immediately, within one second.
> The kitten learns: sitting down means, I will get food.

No clicking detour is needed here! But there isn't any reason, either, why you shouldn't first give a *click* before giving it the food.

Now let us say your half-grown cat has learned quite a bit already, and is sitting in exemplary fashion on the chair in the kitchen rather than doing gymnastics on the dresser, while you have your hands full elsewhere. This is the moment when you can resort at least to symbolic reward and just *click*, so giving a precise symbolic signal of appreciation to reward the cat's correct action, namely its sitting in the proper place. This means you will still have a moment to finish what you are doing, and then organise the real reward which the cat has earned.

The value of this short detour consists in its providing more accurate information to the cat, who registers – or rather, its brain registers – what it is being rewarded for, even if before it gets its treat, half a minute later, it has already jumped down from the chair and is doing something else.

The symbolic reward acts like a snapshot for the brain, with which you have captured the correct action.

Along with the common – and artificial – language that clicker training creates, it also results in an exciting *win-win* situation. We human beings think we are manipulating our cats, and at the same time the cat has the possibility of manipulating us humans in an acceptable and desirable way. This of course is something that cats generally do anyway – but the crucial difference lies in the fact that with the use of clicker training it is all subject to defined rules which we have introduced. The cat thus learns new, successful and at the same time acceptable ways of manipulating us. The bottom line is that it gets more control over its life, without us humans relinquishing control in any way – quite the contrary!

Alongside the learning principle of trial and error, with the ensuing positive consequences – instrumental (or operant) conditioning – there are other learning mechanisms involved as well.

With classical conditioning, links are created between an item of information from the environment in the most extended sense, and an event in the system of the cat. In a practical life context, this learning process gives rise to a simple and above all automatic *if X, then Y* connection:

Two examples:
You present your hungry kitten with a freshly opened can of food. Along with the emotional excitement of joyful anticipation, there are quite a few things going on in the body of the cat – its digestive system gets geared up with all its functions for the coming food, and all in all a positive sense of anticipation is created. For the hungry cat this is a perfectly natural reaction to food – there is nothing else you need to do.
Now add to this situation a certain sound, like the clattering of a spoon on a plate, the rattling of dry food or a whistle, repeating it a number of times, and the cat learns to create a connection: *if* this sound can be heard, *then* it means food! But the useful thing about this learning process is that this positive emotion and pleasurable anticipation will be created even when only the sound is heard, and no food is present.
Of course this kind of classical conditioning can also occur in a negative context – and you will probably be familiar with this example from another cat you had: you fetch the transport box from the basement, and the cat disappears from view immediately. When finally stuffed into the box, it gets sweaty paws, rapid breathing and increased cardiac frequency and feels decidedly unwell. The transport box has become the omen of a negative event, with all the physical and emotional consequences.

The value of this kind of conditioning for the cat is that it makes its life more predictable, because certain stimuli – items of information – which occur simultaneously with bodily events or emotions will presage them in future as well.

And this heralding of a positive event is something you have met just a while back – in connection with clicker training!

The fact is that in reality these two learning mechanisms are inseparably linked with one another:

The cat does something – it hears a click – it gets a reward.
- As a result of classical conditioning, the *click* of symbolic reward and the real reward have become an inseparable pair – *if* the one can be heard, *then* the other is to be expected.
- The action of the cat has a positive consequence in the form of a reward.
- The reward is announced with a *click*.
- The circle of classical conditioning and instrumental conditioning closes.

This close linking of the two kinds of conditioning also reduces the possibility of error in daily training – in the worst case, if you give a *click* by mistake you have passed on inaccurate information, but you have still communicated positive feelings through the reward.

Another very simple learning process which functions quite independently in the everyday life of an emotionally healthy cat is habituation. The cat learns that it doesn't need to react to environmental stimuli that are always there and don't have any kind of significance for it. This may be anything from the traffic at the front of the house to the rustling of a bin bag or music on the radio – everything in the way of noise located in the human environment (but not only there). Simple as this learning process is, it is crucial to the wellbeing of the cat: it simply costs far too much energy to be alert all the time, to react to everything without exception. It is better when the cat's cognitive computing centre has learned through habituation to screen out unimportant things, and only react properly to important items of information.

How cats learn – in practice

In a practical everyday educational context, you use a special noise for clicker training purposes. And as you will soon see, it is very useful and very important to have this noise always on hand. For exceedingly formal training with high aspirations to theoretical correctness and performance, a mechanical object that produces a very distinctive sound – like the eponymous snap-action clicker, for instance, a whistle or similar – can be effective. The problem here occurs when this thing, whether it is a whistle, clicker or pen, is not to hand at the right time when we just want to let the cat know in passing that it really is doing a very good job in whatever it is doing. And just that is much more important, in an educational sense, than teaching the cat a few tricks!

As human beings, in any case, we are fairly skilled in using the mouth as a linguistic tool (when it isn't full, that is) – and the chances of clicking the tongue on the roof of the mouth or the front teeth, or quickly making a characteristic noise with the lips, are pretty favourable. The path from seeing what the cat is doing to thinking that it deserves to be rewarded, and then signalling to the fingers to find a plastic gadget and press it, is considerably longer and less suitable, for informal everyday clicking at least.

The noise you produce doesn't have to be at all loud – quite the reverse, because cats have excellent hearing and are easily startled because they are so sensitive to sound. But it should be distinctive and capable or being duplicated convincingly, so that the cat can actually perceive it and recognise it again subsequently.

> It is very important in this connection to use this tongue noise only – and that means *exclusively* – for this symbolic reward. The sound acquires for the cat a very high information content and value, so it is not a good idea to water down the specific significance by using it to call your cat or clicking just to attract its attention. For this purpose

you would do better to use your cat's name, a whistle or one of the words it is going to learn.

Formal and informal clicking

Formal clicking can be said to cover all set and planned training units where you teach the cat certain exercises or tricks. There is a plan – at least an approximate one – of what you want to teach the cat, and the teaching unit has a start and an end. Apart from the learning effect, formal clicker sessions have high entertainment value, offering the cat variety and the possibility of manipulating us humans in a quite deliberate way. They are a meaningful programme of entertainment for cats of all ages, and are also very suitable as therapy for behaviour problems. The duration of a formal clicker training session will depend on the cat's motivation and level of practice – you can take three to five minutes as a rough indication.

Informal clicking means that you transpose the expertise acquired through joint formal training into an everyday situation. The new language of clicking thus becomes a positive feedback system for the cat. Whenever you want to give positive feedback, you have the right tool available – namely the special noise you make by clicking your tongue. And there are countless possibilities of positive feedback – if you can just get away from the idea of only focusing on the reproachable and prohibited things. The entire catalogue of actions that your cat is naturally permitted to perform suddenly becomes worthy of mention, so that the cat deserves to be rewarded on repeated occasions.

As with formal clicking, the symbolic reward should *always* be followed by a real reward. But in an everyday context there are many different ways of rewarding the cat – it depends on the specific situation.

> **Important: a *click* terminates the action of the cat, and in certain exercises restores the cat's freedom by way of**

reward. So don't expect that after the *click* the cat will go on doing the thing for which you have just rewarded it – the information has arrived nonetheless, and you can restart the exercise at any time.

Classical conditioning in training

By contrast with clicker training, in exercises involving classical conditioning the cat receives the reward during the action and not just subsequently. This simultaneity then gives rise to the positive link between the action and the reward. All exercises where manipulation of the cat's body takes place are suitable occasions for classical conditioning.

Food is the best reward here, because it naturally involves a high degree of motivation, especially when a kitten is hungry enough. The intensity and length of each individual manipulation should only be such that the kitten is still happy and willing to take the food. With all exercises involving classical conditioning, it is important to leave a short pause of 10 to 20 seconds for before repeating the exercise.

What constitutes a reward for cats?

The value of the reward, and the fact that something has the effect of a reward, derive from the fact that the cat actually wants something at this precise moment – and what this is may vary a great deal, depending on the situation.

For a full cat, or one that is not particularly greedy, a treat is not going to present it with an adequate incentive to do something. Likewise when the cat is wound up, stressed or desperate to be let out, food is not going to be effective as a reward. Young and active cats, on the other hand, can well be rewarded with a quick exciting play sequence. Other equally attractive possibilities, following a not particularly appreciated manipulation like nail trimming or grooming, are an opening door, the exploration of new things or places or just letting the cat have its freedom again.

It depends on the cat's mood and current needs, and the situation generally, what is going to have a rewarding effect for the cat. Here the important thing is that we humans should observe, learn and experiment creatively, in order to discover what constitutes a reward for our cat in its momentary situation:

- Ordinary dry food
- Proper pieces of meat
- Dried meat
- Solid, creamy or liquid treats of all kinds
- Ham
- Liver pâté
- Cheese
- Salmon
- Yogurt or cream cheese
- Pudding
- Croissants
- 30 second play session
- Starting a game after a pause
- Letting go or stopping
- Opening a door
- Catnip
- Valerian
- ...

All real food rewards should be small to minute – you don't want the cat to be full and satisfied after the third mouthful of treat, and you don't want it to be focused on eating for too long either, it should be interested in getting more. For solid treats an edge length of 3 to 5 mm (0,1 – 0,2 in) is appropriate, with liquid treats three licks should suffice – and this is also an opportunity for kittens to learn how to lick from a spoon.

Indira gets a reward, and learns at the same time how to get something off a spoon.

Less material rewards, but not to be underestimated, are undivided attention, praise and acknowledgement, contact, information and satisfying the cat's curiosity – any of these, depending on the situation, can have a higher value than rewards in the form of food.

For clicker training, the following basic rule applies:

> **Every *click* you make means in principle that it will *always* be followed by at least one real reward.**

In everyday, informal training on the other hand, it may occasionally happen that a *click* has to stand in its own right, because the cat doesn't take its reward, or because the situation really is such that no reward apart from positive acknowledgement is possible at the time. The *click* and the information will certainly be registered by the cat, but be aware that every *solo click* that is not followed by a real reward is in a way a broken promise.

Depending on how eagerly the cat was expecting something, this can certainly have the effect of reducing its motivation in future – above all if it happens frequently.

The first three exercises

You can, and should start with the first training session as soon as the kitten, having just arrived, has had time to look around, made itself more or less at home, is hungry from the many new impressions or is still lively enough to enjoy a game.

All three basic exercises work with 'targets' – simple goal points which the cat has to touch, in order to get a *click* and then the rewarding experience that signals success. With these targets, which can later be combined in any way you like, you have all the possibilities you need of steering your cat in an educational sense – in the direction, that is to say, of one of these targets.

Nose target

This first and simplest of all exercises fulfils several functions at once. First of all it is easy to learn, because it relies on the natural reaction of all cats to touch an outstretched finger with their nose. And then too, this super-easy – but very meaningful – action teaches the cat the meaning of the tongue click, coming to associate the sound with a real reward.

> **The kitten learns how learning works, and discovers that information from human beings is important and valuable!**

The nose target is thus the basis of **all** exercises, and whenever you or the cat have a momentary low, getting back to the very first familiar baby exercise of the nose target will always be found helpful. In later life the nose target can also be used as a leading or pointing exercise – you can lead the cat with your finger anywhere you want it to go, show it the way or point the way, if you want to teach it more tricks or show it to a place. In crisis situations, to back up your calling to the cat, and also on visits to the vet, a well learned nose target can have a relaxing effect, communicate security and rebuild confidence.

Skyboy already does a perfect nose target.

The nose target is your outstretched index finger – at the cat's height, and held to start with at about 5 to 10 centimetres (2 - 4 in) from the cat's nose. The moment the cat nudges your finger with its nose, you make your special tongue click and give the cat a small reward like a tiny bit of food, let the cat lick yogurt off a different finger from the one you have been using as a target or give the cat an interactive play session of 20 to 30 seconds.

After two or three tries, many kittens will lose interest in this new target game and will look for a more direct way of getting at the reward – without this stupid nudging game, which they see as a pointless detour, or they will simply stop and wander off. Then you should change to the next target or have a break, until the cat is hungry again and sufficiently motivated.

When your kitten starts to use its paws on the nose target, move on immediately to the next exercise, the paws target. If no paws come into play, but the cat is still motivated and hungry enough, switch to exercise 3, the sitting target.

Paw target

As soon as your cat shows an inclination to touch the nose target with its forepaws instead of with its nose, open your hand and offer the vertical or horizontal palm of your hand as a contact surface for the paw. At the moment it doesn't make any difference how exactly the cat carries out the exercise – it is just a matter of learning the difference between *nose touching the finger* and *paw touching the palm*.

In this initial phase of target training, you can – and should – actually adapt the target to suit the action: that is to say, when the cat approaches with its paw, you offer the palm; when it comes with its nose, you proffer the finger. Only when, after a number of repetitions, the kitten has really grasped the difference, can you remain insistent and click and reward the cat only when the right action for the target is selected.

One possibility of getting the cat motivated for this game is a somewhat higher sitting place on an edge, for example on a table – and coming from below with the palm, at such a distance that it is more easily reached with the paw than with the nose. The first lifting of the paw will then at once be rewarded with a *click*. When the cat gradually gets the point, the palm comes closer so that the paw can touch it – the paw target is complete.

Based on the paw target exercise you can later develop tricks like *gimme five* or *high five* or indeed *ten* with two paws, if it takes your fancy.

An upturned cup with food underneath it, as a further way of practising the paw target, would be a way of moving on to the shell game. Or if you are brave enough, you could teach your cat another paw target like the light switch…

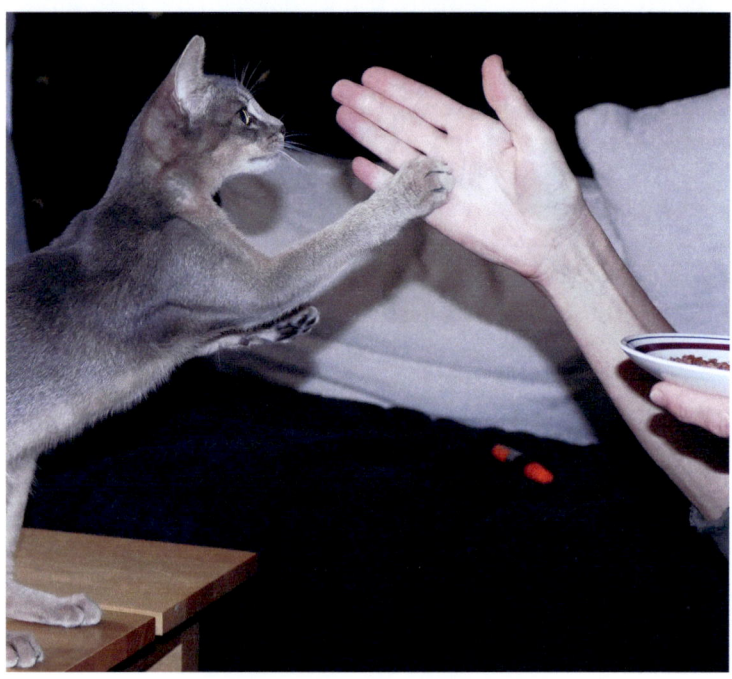

Sunnyboy shows a controlled paw target.

Sitting target

A third, very simple basic exercise, which relies on the cat's natural enthusiasm for sitting in small boxes or walking on a limited defined surface, like a newspaper or a blanket.

Place a small box between yourself and the cat and be on the ready – many kittens will respond to the invitation and jump in immediately. Mark the cat's jumping in with a *click*, and give the cat its reward *outside* the box. After the reward has been consumed, encourage your cat to jump into the box again – here you could also use the nose target which it has learned already. Likewise the second to fifth reward will be given to the cat *outside* the box. This is because the current exercise is still called *Get in the box*.

While the game has not yet palled, and your little bundle of energy is still eagerly jumping into the box, from now on it gets its *click* and reward *while* it is sitting in the box. The exercise assignment has just changed slightly, and is now S*it in the box*. You can increase the time that you want the cat to sit in the box progressively – cats naturally have a lot of persistence and patience when they sit somewhere or when they want something. You have now succeeded in steering this persistence into meaningful channels, with the help of the box, and the quiet sitting of the cat becomes 'loud' – in the sense of conspicuous – in that it happens in a special place which has our attention. Whenever your kitten wants something – even if it is just the next meal – you should consistently invite it to jump in the box and sit there, and then – *click*, there is the food or the game or whatever the kitten was wanting. Once the kitten has grasped this exercise, at some point it is going to sit in the box of its own accord in order to see what will happen – and you mustn't let this moment pass, but should acknowledge it with a generous reward!

In the long term, you see, this sitting target is going to turn into the *wish box*, where the cat's wishes come true if it just sits properly in the box and waits. The great majority of cats will naturally use the wish box most commonly in order to ask for food. But if you want, you can certainly use it in other situations as well, and ask your cat, with the help of the terms it has learned, whether it wants to *eat, play* or *go out* for example.

If you are afraid that from now on the cat will spend all its time sitting in the wish box, you don't really need to worry – on the one hand cats are in any case very persistent and patient – when sitting in the wish box as well – and on the other, a certain randomness of the reward (resulting from the everyday situation) is the best guarantee of the exercise continuing to work in the long term.

Many cats will start to find an exercise boring, above all at the beginning, after just a few repetitions – not because they don't understand it, but on the contrary, because they get the point so quickly. Here it helps if after three to five repetitions you introduce a different exercise, or take a break. But there are certainly kittens who are capable of learning the basics of these three target exercises, and even a few things more, in the very first training session. What they don't always see so quickly, however, is the reason why they should cooperate at all.

With your consistent patience and regular training sessions (one to three times daily, each lasting a few minutes), the most stubborn young cats will learn that even for cute midgets like themselves, life is not going to offer a free lunch without a minimum of cooperation on their part. Whether they learn this lesson in their natural cat life outdoors, when hunting mice, or from sitting in the wish box indoors, doesn't make all that much difference in the end: a job is a job.

Once your young cat has grasped, after two or three days, what will most rapidly result in success, at any time when your cat wants something you can always call for one of the three target exercises, or even a combination:

It's time for a meal – just take a few seconds to do the exercise with the wish box, the cat gets its *click* and dinner is served.

Or if a play session gets too wild and out of control – here a short break to restore bearings and self-possession can be helpful, just touch the nose target and then the game can be resumed. The young cat finds it easy to learn the principle that it has to *do* something, to carry out some small action, in order to reach the desired goal.

In the kitten kindergarten it has only taken Xerox a few minutes to learn that the sitting target is his wish box.

Other important exercises for everyday

Every use of human language is subject to the principle that human words or names on the face of it have no meaning whatever to cats. They only learn from repetitions of certain situations to make a connection, and match the sound to the act. So if you want to give your cat an inkling of the significance of human vocabulary, it is essential to link an action, a place, a person or another cat, an object or a situation with the word. Only after a number of repetitions does it mean something to the cat – though exactly what idea it forms of this word, unfortunately, will never really be fathomable by us. But experience shows that cats can acquire a quite passable vocabulary, and can even learn whole sentences, and the information they acquire proves very helpful to them in everyday life.

Its own name

Kittens will soonest learn that their name must have something to do with them if you speak it every time you have contact, every time you look at your cat or it looks at you. Only after this first phase of interaction does it make sense to call the cat by its name, if at the time it is otherwise engaged. If it reacts – even if just with a small twitch of the ears or turn of the head – that is a good sign that it is starting to get the point.

Ideal friendly-sounding cat names, incidentally, will have one or two syllables, and will contain one or two Is or Ys and not too many sharp hissing consonants like S.

Coming when called or whistled for

Cats are well able to respond to the command *Come*, or even to a whistle – after all, they do show up pretty quickly when they hear an enticing sound like the opening of a tin or the fridge door, or any other sound suggesting positive consequences. The difference is that between systematic training and learning by accident. Come gains its meaning if you call the cat with *Come* (or *Come to me*) – and if you like later on with a whistle – as soon as the cat comes to you of its own accord. It makes no difference whether its approaching you is purely coincidental, whether you have a toy or food in your hand or the cat is already responding to its name and comes to you for that reason. At all events you only say *Come* when the cat is actually coming – this is the only way the cat's perception will link the behaviour of *coming to you* with the word *Come*. Of course it is helpful if you receive the cat with a *click* and something extra special – a straight meal, a small treat or a short game. And just petting can be an effective reward for many cats in this situation.

You can turn a normal mealtime routine into an intensive learning session, by calling your hungry kitten with *Come*, giving it a small morsel and while it is eating shifting your position – as soon as it is finished, you call it again, and so carry on until it has worked its way right through the meal.

Once you are reasonably confident that the cat knows what *Come* means – 5 to 10 repetitions may already be enough for this – you can try actually calling it when it is out of sight. You can make an excellent learning game out of this, if you have a large apartment or house and the cat is already allowed out into the garden, or in case of learning excursions, into strange apartments. You quietly go into another room or to a different story, or hide somewhere, and call the cat from here. If it comes galloping up to you, it immediately gets a click and a super reward. If the cat is too quick to follow you, get somebody to hold it or give it a few treats to divert its attention while you hide, and then call it.

In the initial phase you don't want to have too much distraction from strange surroundings or other activities, because the more often you say *Come* and the cat doesn't come to you, the sooner it will forget the meaning it has learned already. You will then find yourself in the same position as many dog owners, whose dogs come when they are called – or perhaps don't.

Once the cat comes when called, you can practise the same sequence with a whistle added: you hide – call the cat's name, whistle – *click* and a nice reward. After a few repetitions, the whistle alone will be enough. With the whistle in particular it is useful to work with exceptionally tasty treats, rather than using it just for daily calling purposes and trivialities – in this way it becomes a highly reliable signal, which the cat will almost always respond to with enthusiasm.

Lifting up

Kittens who have not learned in the first few weeks of life that it is normal to be picked up and carried, often try by struggling to get their paws back down on the floor. Even if this learning process cannot really be made up for so that they will actually like being carried, you can still teach a kitten like this to tolerate being lifted up and carried at least.

> **NB: the crucial thing in this learning game is that the quickest way back to the floor is never struggling, but always relaxation. This however means that the training steps have to be quite small, so that you stay just within the comfort zone of your kitten and it gets back to the floor before it tries to get free. Otherwise it will learn the exact opposite of what we want to teach it, that is to say *The more I struggle and fight, the sooner I will be put down.***

Always be careful when carrying untrained kittens to support the whole body effectively, and so give them a feeling of confidence. For more sensitive young cats, it may be sensible to start the training with even smaller steps, by first just putting a hand under their rib cage; lifting the body of the cat, while leaving its paws on the floor; lifting the front paws off the floor while the hind paws still touch the floor; and finally lifting the whole kitten a few centimetres up in the air, and putting it down on the floor again immediately. Each of these individual steps will be rewarded with a *click* and a real reward, and repeated a sufficient number of times till the kitten is able to remain relaxed and in an attitude of positive expectation. Give your cat a word each time, like *Carry*, as a forewarning of this kind of manipulation.

Lifting down from above likewise only becomes a relaxed operation which the cat can take for granted, when it has learned to trust its human in this situation from an early stage.

Lifting down from above

Even kittens that are quite capable of being picked up and carried without a problem often have to learn that they can lifted down from above, not just the other way around. To practise this, put your kitten in a place where it is higher than you. Then lift it down to you, quite slowly and while maintaining control. Some cats like leaning on their front paws. After a few repetitions, this will have become so much a part of the cat's fund of experience that it will remember as an adult in later life, and will let itself be lifted down from high altitudes without panicking and resorting to its claws.

Sitting

Any cat can sit, and in case of doubt it will actually do it extremely persistently, in most cases more readily, in fact, than a puppy – so it should be an easy matter to teach the cat to *Sit*! To begin with it is simpler to wait until the cat sits, and just reward it for sitting because *Sit* doesn't as yet mean anything to the cat. At some point even the liveliest kitten is going to sit down – and then you can go *click* (optional) and reward it immediately.

Another possibility is to hold out a small treat in your fingers, in front of the cat's nose and then moving it in the direction of the back of the head, so that the easiest and most convenient way for the cat to reach it is by sitting down. The moment its bottom goes down, open your fingers and let the cat eat the treat in seated position.

But be careful – if you hold the food too high in your fingers, the cat will try to jump up at it, do an uncontrolled *Sit Pretty* (see below) or reach for it with its paws, possibly roughly. In order to do this exercise, moreover, it should already be able to take food from your fingers in a controlled way and without mistake. There are cats who are very solution-oriented, and these will always try the shortest route rather than sitting down, so with them this exercise is unlikely to work in this way.

With very demanding cats, you can back up the exercise with a *click* (if the cat is familiar with the target exercises) – the cat who is not diverted by the food will then sit down eventually of its own accord. Then you can click and produce the treat, in order to avoid the preceding agitation.

Only when the cat offers to sit almost automatically in many situations can you start to introduce the command *Sit* or *Sit down*! You look on while your kitten sits down right in front of you, and every time it does this, you say *Sit down*. This gives the act of sitting a verbal label, which you can use in future in order to tell your cat to sit. As with the wish box, you can now extend the duration of sitting, by testing the patience of the cat just as far as it can go, so that it stays sitting down and doesn't get up again out of frustration.

Eye contact

Looking into our eyes and maintaining eye contact can be a useful exercise. This looking activity enables the cat to be seen and get attention, it supports the exchange of information (e.g. about how the cat is feeling or what is currently going on), and in addition it encourages social bonding. From studies involving humans and dogs it is known that eye contact actually causes the hormone oxytocin to be released. This hormone strengthens the sense of social security and cohesion. Although there have not been any similar studies of the cat to human relationship to date, there is actually no reason not to believe that eye contact here has a similar effect. On us human beings certainly! The exercise can also be useful if you want to take portrait photos of cats (without a long-distance lens), because there are a great many cats who are fundamentally inclined to look away when you try to photograph them.

For cats it really does amount to a learning process to hold a person's gaze, because in cat interactions it is a threat, or at least grossly impolite, to look directly for a long time or actually stare at another cat.

So for this exercise a few basic rules have to be kept in mind:
- Keep your expression gentle at all times

- Blink frequently at intervals
- In doing this exercise, maintain a polite distance of about one metre
- Reward your cat, even for quite short moments of success, by giving a *click* and then rewarding it in the real form of a treat or a game.

In order to create eye contact in the first place you can make subtle noises (not a *click!*) or hold something interesting, like food or a toy, in the line of vision between your eyes and those of the seated cat. This invitation can then be gradually relinquished, being replaced by a gesture with the index finger and/or the command *Look* (or *Look at me*).

Confined sitting

Sitting can be introduced as a simple default position or preprogrammed basic position for a great many manipulations – from now on, anything you want to get the cat to do will always start from a default *Sit*. For this purpose the exercise must be extended into one involving confined sitting – here the cat is restricted by your hands, a rolled towel or its surroundings, but not actually pinned down. The cat should learn to sit more or less voluntarily – for example, for a veterinary examination or for the administration of tablets – because the physical limitation effectively prevents the cat's typical evasive action of scrabbling backwards.

There are many possible forms of this confined sitting exercise:
- The seated kitten is confined with a hand on its back, just above its tail, and with the other hand on the front of its chest
- A big towel is rolled up and arranged so as to surround the kitten
- The kitten sits in the corner of the sofa or in a small box

- The kitten sits back to front between your thighs while you kneel.

Sunnyboy sits in a relaxed way without being pinned down, just slightly confined by the hands.

This restrictive, but not completely immobilising position can be used as a basis for checking or brushing the cat's teeth, giving it eyedrops or tablets or carrying out other therapeutic interventions. Here of course it is essential that you proceed slowly and systematically, with every single tiny success in the development of tolerance and keeping still being rewarded with a symbolic *click*, followed by a real treat subsequently. Alternatively you can teach this exercise on the basis of classical conditioning, by giving the kitten food for as long as it remains restricted (pastes are a good choice here), the food then disappearing along with the confining hands. What the kitten learns from this is – *I'm not all that fond of having hands on me, but they always mean delicious food, well then, I'll take the complete package…*

Sitting in a specific place

Another extension of the cat's sitting ability is to get it to sit in a specific place. If the kitchen dresser or dining table has been seriously declared out of bounds, then the kitten should be given a different place right from the start close to these taboo zones, from which it can reach all those fabulous exciting things which it expects to get at by jumping on the table or dresser. In this way you avoid the all too frequent educational misunderstanding where the cat is just told *not* to do something, without being given an acceptable alternative option. Unless the cat acquires a new behavioural pattern (a much more successful one, because it earns rewards), the frustrating game of 'cat jumps up – gets pushed down – jumps up again' will go on for a long time, putting an unnecessary strain on the relationship.

Basically this exercise is simply concerned to set up another target for sitting, just like the wish box. So whenever the cat wants to be involved, when treats are about to be distributed or other activities are on the agenda, where it is better that the cat remain at a distance as an observer – you can invite the kitten to sit in *its* place. You can manage this most effectively by luring the kitten in a certain direction with the nose target, or by placing treats regularly in these places, or only giving your cat treats at such spots.

And of course there is no reason why you shouldn't set up a number of these places for sitting, if needed, at intervals around the house. If this *Go to your place* or *On your mark* has been well trained on a regular basis, and properly rewarded, it becomes a reliable ritual, and can quickly be used to restore a feeling of safety and confidence – for example in case of conflict between cats, tension and stress or the introduction of a new cat.

Exercises of this kind stabilise the cat's everyday routine, because they become predictable fixed points in the time - space - social system of the cat. In case of any kind of confusion, insecurity or disturbance of the everyday, you can easily get the cat or cats slotted back into a safe daily routine by inviting them to their places.

Go to your places: *Windy Whisper and Fiji File sit in their places – a stable ritual which creates confidence and security.*

Lying on the side

Voluntarily lying on its side can be a quite useful exercise if you need to examine a cat – eyes, ears, teeth, paws and of course the rest of the body. As this lateral recumbent position gives inexperienced cats the unpleasant feeling of having lost control, it makes sense to show them at a very early stage that the experience is quite a normal one. It is important for this exercise, at all events, to have a very soft underlay and a rather relaxed young cat, who is not going to be active in full play mode when you make the first attempts. Lay your kitten, in a friendly and careful way but still definitely, on its side, and pin in down just to such an extent that it cannot get up from this lateral position. Well educated kittens know from their mother perfectly well about holding still in this position, they may not yet have quite grasped that we want the same thing from them. So reward just the first second of keeping still in lateral position with a *click*, letting the kitten go immediately and then giving it a real reward in the form of food or a play. Don't overdo it, and leave off after two or three exercise units, to avoid engendering negative emotions. Depending on how well your kitten succeeds in keeping still, you can either reduce the pressure quite gradually with which you are holding it down, or prolong the time of keeping still. The perfect outcome of the exercise will be a cat that lies freely and fully relaxed on its side, and waits trustingly until it hears your *click*. Change the side from time to time, in order to incorporate both positions in the cat's horizon of experience.

As with confined sitting, here too you would also have the possibility of classical conditioning, where you let your kitten lick a paste as long as it stays lying down; when it comes out of the lateral position, the food disappears. The handling becomes more complicated, however, when you have a twitchy kitten and have to hold onto a tube of paste at the same time.

As with all other exercises, it is important that your kitten should never be frightened, or resist violently, when doing the exercise. If this happens, stop immediately, and go back a few steps to simpler learning games like the target exercises, sitting or confined sitting.

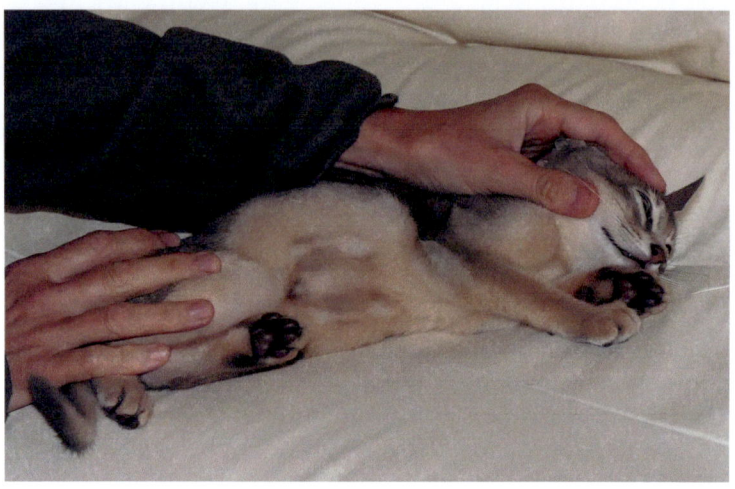

Lying on his side (to begin with in a slightly restricted way, and later voluntarily) is a useful exercise, which Sunnyboy is learning here on a soft underlay.

Lying on the back

After lying on its side, the logical next step for the kitten is lying on its back – and there are also some practical grounds for learning this position: trimming nails, examining its tummy and grooming, or if necessary, even an X-ray or ultrasound investigation.

The procedure is the same as with lying on the side. This time the soft underlay can be the hollow between your thighs or a rolled-up blanket, which gives the kitten stability to the side. For relaxed kittens who like to be tickled on their belly this exercise will not present great difficulties – they will take to it at once. With kittens who don't mind about the loss of control this position involves, you can start to reward them after the very first second, or if necessary even half a second of lying on their back. As with the side position, classical conditioning is a little bit more complicated, but is a good way to give the supine position a positive flavour. It is not realistic to expect to achieve free and relaxed lying on the back with all cats, but being familiar with the situation still robs the situation of the panic factor, if at any time it should become necessary.

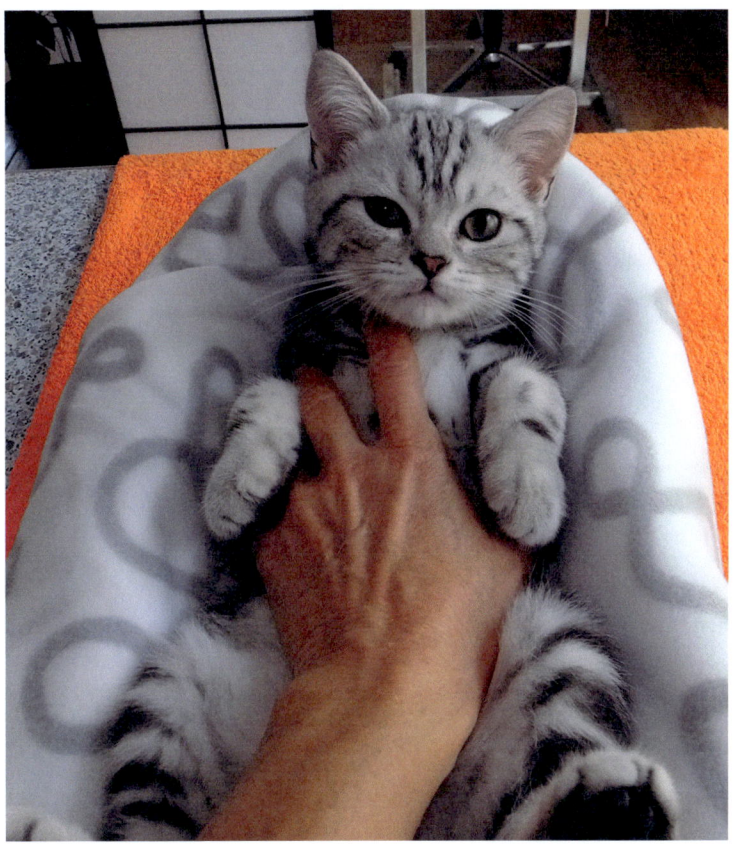

With a soft blanket as a stable surround, Xerox has learned how to lie on his back in the kitten kindergarten – and he knows already that a reward can be expected.

Tolerance for handling and personal care

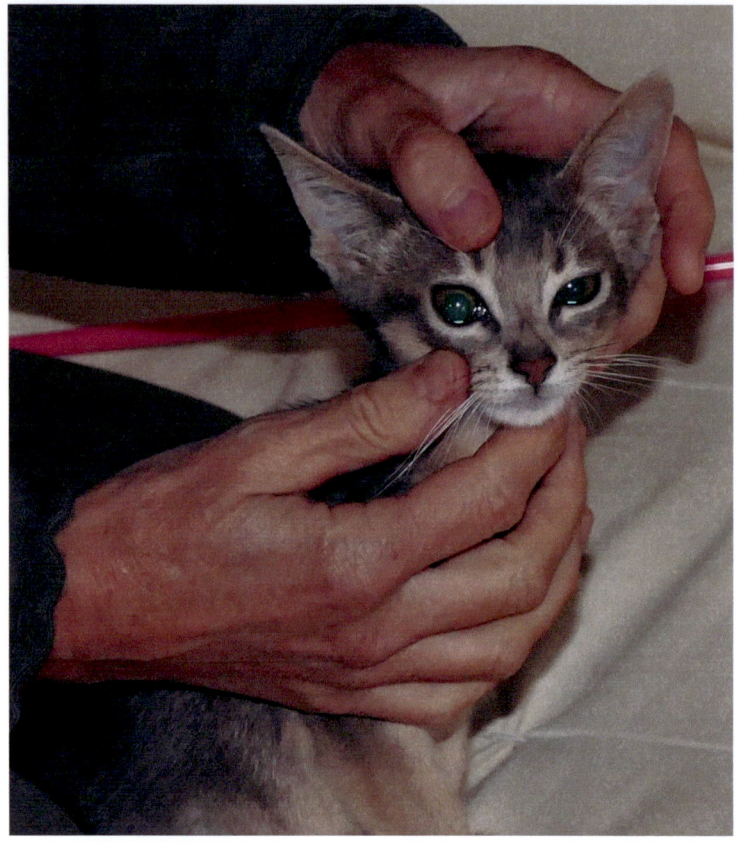

Tolerating the examination of eyes, ears and nose should be something that every cat takes for granted – as Sunnyboy demonstrates here in a confined sitting position.

For kittens it is not immediately obvious why they should be manipulated and groomed by human beings – actually they can do this kind of thing well enough unaided. In principle, of course, this is perfectly correct – cats do clean themselves, and look after their claws... and as for swallowing tablets, that is nothing to worry about. That is just going to happen somehow or other... automatically... one presumes...

Unfortunately this no longer applies to the grooming of semi-long-haired or long-haired cats – and the health of teeth and gums is also likely to be more or less adversely affected in 70% of cats aged three years or more. The older a cat gets, the more personal care it needs – so it can be a considerable advantage if you observe the principle of *starting them young*, and establish this kind of routine as automatic in the first few weeks of the cat's life.

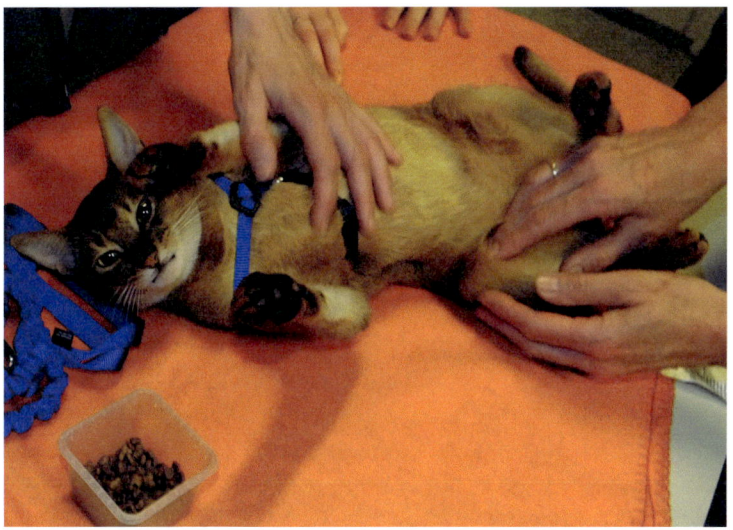

Windy Whisper is able to work as a model on the First Aid course, because he has learned to allow all his bodily areas to be touched for some time – of course only because he spies the prospect of something nice to come.

Not all cats are equally tolerant of human handling and personal care. And whereas this kind of training presents no very great difficulties with well socialised and tolerant kittens, when you have to do with little feral cats, who have grown up without any trusting contact with human beings, a really demanding programme of exercises may be required. Although these resistant and intolerant kittens may challenge you to relax or abandon their education – not to mention causing you a certain amount of frustration along the way – it is these cats above all who are probably going to benefit from it the most at a later stage.

The most important rule is to proceed slowly and patiently. You are most likely to get cooperation from a cat when you have all the time in the world – or at least act as if this were the case!

Compulsion that the cat finds incomprehensible can even lose you the open friendliness of a tolerant cat, if the cat can see no benefit to be derived from the deal.

To begin with it makes sense to get clear how far kitten can already tolerate being touched, or put up with certain physical positions – like confined sitting, or simply lying on its side. The moment just *before* it finds something uncomfortable and resists is your starting line. Then too you should have a clear picture of what you want your final target to be. And the path from A to B should then be broken down into lots of tiny, minute steps, which you can reward with a *click* and whatever the cat fancies after that. This plan is effective, as is an inner attitude of cheerful but determined resolution – by contrast with hesitation, which will often encourage the cat to resist.

With all these exercises, regular repetitions until the cat reaches adulthood are advisable, because there are certainly some young cats who are tolerant up till the age of puberty, but who then start to see certain bodily areas as private and so are reluctant for them to be touched by a human being.

Grooming

Your fluffy kitten is just about able to tolerate being combed twice on its back – and you know that as a long-haired cat it will be needing regular grooming (including in intimate zones, like the tummy and inner thigh) in a few months.

You start with a well hungry (and so really motivated) kitten, and begin by grooming it twice on the back in a confined sitting position, commenting on the procedure in your own words (for example, *grooming time*), and click at the end of the sequence; kitten receives a small reward, relax. Back to the default position with *Sit* and again groom through the kitten's fur twice, click and reward. After 3 to 5 repetitions you can either raise it to three passes of the comb, or instead change the position – for example, moving towards the side of the rib cage or front of the chest. With each exercise you can gradually raise the goal, either in terms of the duration or in what concerns the bodily areas touched – but never both at the same time! That is to say, either groom more often, or extend the range to include more sensitive areas as well, and revert again to just one or two passes of the comb.

Important: an exercise session should always end when things are going really well, not when the cat tells you it's had enough!

An elegant alternative version may be used, best practised with the help of a second person. Here the kitten learns on the basis of classical conditioning that it *only* gets treats along with grooming and at the same time – either both together, or nothing at all. So you apply the comb – while holding a treat under its nose. The timing of this procedure however needs to be very precise, so that the cat can really recognise the connection between the two variables. Between repetitions, which to start with will of course only take up a few seconds, the cat needs a short pause for reflection. So start and finish the grooming and feeding simultaneously – followed by a few seconds for reflection – then groom and feed again, etc.

Particularly suitable for this exercise are cat pâtés and creamy treats which the cat can lick from the tube, from a spoon, spatula or small disposable syringe (you can get these from a pharmacy or from your vet).

Both strategies – clicking to reward tolerance, or the simultaneous (and hence linked) offer of manipulation and treats – can obviously be extended to all other kinds of handling and interventions for personal care. All these exercises will be very much easier for kittens if you carry them out on a soft blanket as underlay. The individual steps could be something along the following lines:

- **Touching taboo zones**: here the kitten should be able to recognise that it is getting a particularly good deal, and it is extremely important to proceed slowly and politely. Especially sensitive zones are the belly, the groin, the back of the thigh and the anogenital region.

Nail trimming

On the face of it, trimming the cat's nails is not essential – but it can make living with cats a whole lot easier. Simply curtailing the razor-sharp tips of the claws does not hurt, and will not affect the free-roaming cat adversely either – but it does reduce the frequency of inadvertent and unpleasant scratches, when a young cat gets too boisterous in playing, tries to catch onto its human or use you as a launching pad.

As cats' claws, like fingernails, continue to grow all the time, in just a week the sharp tips will be back again. Nail trimmers for cats should be as small, sharp and quiet as possible.

Trimming nails begins with the starting position *Sit*. Depending on how tolerant the young cat is, it can be rewarded just for letting you hold its paw, letting you exert slight pressure on the toes to make the claws project, touch them with a little nail trimmer and finally pinch off the claw tips. The final goal is to curtail all the claws of the front paws, and then with a *click* dispense the appropriate reward – letting the cat go again, giving it a treat or a game.

A second possibility for nail trimming is to do it when the cat is lying on its back. Apart from the kitten's position, the procedure remains exactly the same.

If you are uncertain about any of these manoeuvres or about the right length to cut, you can get your vet to show you the individual steps and the right way of trimming the cat's nails.

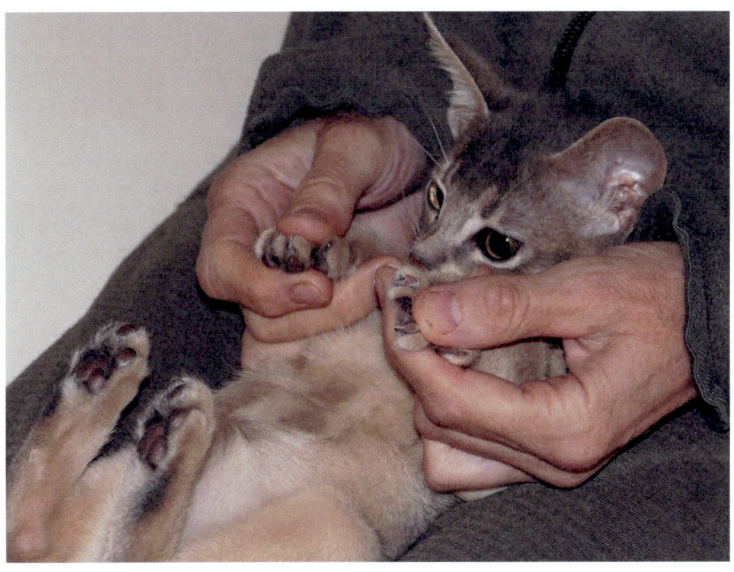

A preliminary exercise for nail trimming – lying in stable position on his back, Sunnyboy allows his paws to be touched and toes stretched so as to extend the claws.

Giving tablets

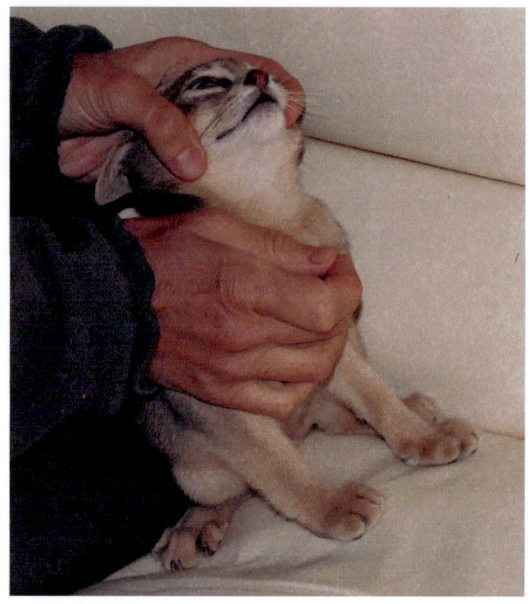

In order to take tablets, Sunnyboy has already learned confined sitting, and now lets his head be turned in a relaxed way, until his nose is pointing vertically upwards.

The problems of administering tablets to cats are practically legendary! And yet it is so simple to teach a young cat, in just a few practice sessions, that swallowing tablets is a perfectly normal interaction with human beings.

The default position, as so often, is *Sit*, ideally confined so that the cat cannot pull away – in a small box or corner of the sofa, or parked back to front between the thighs in kneeling position.

You show the cat a few small treats, such as dry food for kittens, ham or cheese cubes in tablet size, and then give it one or two along with the information *Tablet* or *Candy* or *Goody*.

Then grasp the kitten's head, coming from above and from the front and holding the cheekbone on both sides with your thumb and index finger, while your little finger rests on the back of the kitten's head. So the whole of the kitten's small head is resting in your hand – and don't worry, it isn't going to break! If your kitten reacts with a great deal of sensitivity, you can now give it a *click* for the first time and then one of the dummy pills you have prepared as a reward, with a few repetitions until the cat is OK with the handling.

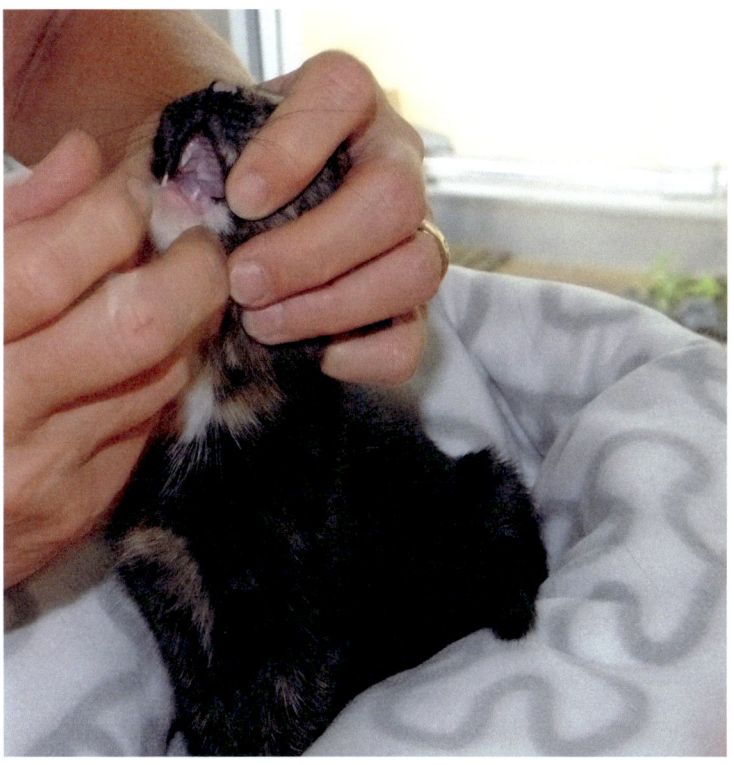

When you turn the head, the tension of the jaw automatically relaxes and you can easily drop the treat (which you have declared to be a 'tablet') into the cat's open mouth.

The next step is to turn the kitten's head back so that the nostrils really point directly upwards – and for this unfamiliar position as well, the cat will immediately get a *click* and a reward. On no account should you try to break the kitten's resistance, if it does resist, by exerting more pressure – just maintain the position resolutely, until after a few seconds the cat relaxes again. Whenever the exercise breaks down with struggling on the kitten's part, a simple rule applies: just go back to the start – *Sit* – and begin again, proceeding this time very much more slowly and in smaller sub-steps.

Once the head of the cat is stretched so far back that its nose is pointing directly upwards, the tension of the jaw automatically relaxes – some cats will open their mouths wide, others just a few millimetres. You take advantage of any hint of opening, and drop one of the tablets/treats into the cat's mouth. Then you can immediately give another click, let the cat's head go and offer it the next treat at once, for eating without interference.

It doesn't actually matter too much whether the cat swallows perfectly the first time, or continues to chew on the treat – there are many more repetitions to look forward to. Along with the treats/tablets, you can also practice with empty capsules (obtainable from the pharmacy). These capsules are already somewhat larger, and can be stuffed or prepared with all kinds of good things before being used for the exercise.

The important thing is that you develop a relaxed routine with your cat – holding the cat firmly, turning the head and dropping something in its mouth – without frightening the cat and without any loss of trust.

The result of this exercise with dummy pills is that the cat no longer questions what is going in its mouth, but first just swallows and then looks for more treats.

> **NB: on no account should you fumble around in the kitten's mouth with your fingers – human fingers are much too big for kittens, and bad experiences with this exercise will never be forgotten.**

For the same reason, you should not exaggerate the frequency of this exercise – three times a day is really enough. Once you have got the procedure running smoothly, you will only need the occasional playful repetition every few weeks.

Da Vinci learns with the help of a small disposable syringe how to take liquid preparations.

The administration of liquids works similarly, with one important difference – you mustn't stretch the cat's head back, or there is a risk of choking.

Fill a small disposable syringe (1 ml or 2 ml syringe, obtainable from your vet or pharmacy) with tasty liquid snacks, pudding or similar and start by letting the cat lick it, as with the grooming exercise. You introduce the syringe with the cat's head in normal position (that is more or less looking straight ahead) by inserting it from the side between the teeth.

Whenever you get the feeling that your kitten doesn't really grasp what is going on or shows a tendency to resist, make the individual steps of the procedure quite tiny, and repeat each one with a *click* as confirmation and reward before you go on. Above all for more sensitive kittens it helps if you carry out a lot of very short practice sessions at intervals of one day, rather than too frequent repetitions in one training unit. Take care to choose times for these exercises when your young cat is not too actively wound up, but well motivated and fairly relaxed.

Brushing teeth

Brushing a cat's teeth may sound a bit overdone, but in view of the incredible frequency of problems involving teeth and inflammation of the gums, this most definitely is not the case. And when you start with a young cat, you have the best chance of clicking your simple measure of medical prophylaxis into an established place in the cat's routine, so that it comes to be accepted as the most normal thing in the world. Even if in the last resort you don't manage to brush your cat's teeth regularly once a day, when practised with a young cat this exercise nonetheless forms a basis for getting the cat to let you inspect and check its teeth and gums later on without protesting.

For brushing teeth you again use the default position *Sit* with a restriction behind, as when giving tablets. If you are fit enough, parking the cat backwards between your thighs again offers you one of the simplest positions for the procedure.

As when administering tablets, you hold the cat's head frontally from above, smoothing back the whiskers with index finger and thumb. When your thumb reaches the corner of the cat's mouth, pull it back and up in such a way that the teeth of the upper jaw come into view. Try to find the best spot on the side of the upper lip, in order to expose as many teeth as possible.

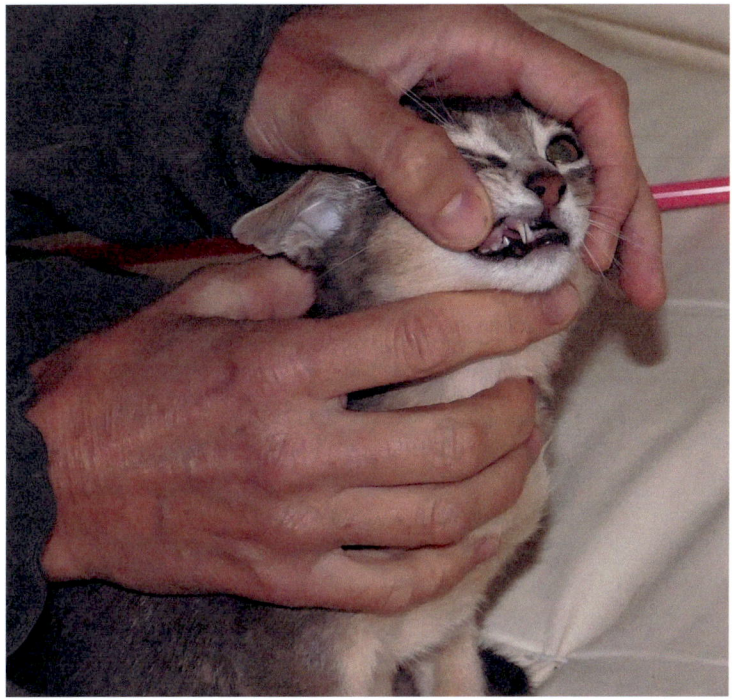

The preliminary exercise for tooth brushing starts from a confined sitting position: you lift the lips, inspect and gently touch the teeth with the finger or a cotton bud.

Kittens have 24 milk teeth, which they change in the period from the 12th week to approximately the 6th month of life, after which as adult cats they have a complete set of 30 teeth.

Until the change of teeth is complete, the tiny milk teeth do not have to be brushed too seriously – up to this point, this is just a playful phase of habituation. The oral cavity of baby cats is moreover still very small, and they are not very willing in the first place to tolerate manipulations of this kind. The change of teeth actually causes some young cats a certain amount of discomfort – even if the cat, in the nature of things, does not make a great deal of fuss about the symptoms. In particular, when the molars at the back come through this often causes an inflammation of the gingiva, so any attempt to brush the teeth would be painful and unpleasant.

But of course manipulation as such can be practised from a very early stage, with the help of cotton buds as a substitute for the toothbrush and a pleasantly tasting cat's toothpaste.

Once a young cat can sit still and is able to tolerate the lifting of its lips, you can apply a little toothpaste gently, using your finger or a cotton bud. The pleasant taste of these special toothpastes in itself constitutes an incentive, but of course you can give a click as well and reinforce the lesson with further rewards. Cotton buds are small enough to be used as practice toothbrushes, so that the young cat gradually learns to tolerate having its teeth and gums touched.

The second half of the jaw is easy to reach, if you turn the cat's head slightly towards you, change your grip so that the thumb is again close to the left corner of the mouth and able to pull the lip up and back. The little incisors can be reached directly from the front.

An alternative position for tooth brushing is to have the cat lying on its side – here of course it is important that the cat should already have learned to lie down in a relaxed way. This position offers somewhat more stability all round, because the head lies on its side and does not need to be held; as in the sitting position, the lips can be pushed back or up from the corner of the mouth, using the thumb or index finger.

It is essential when brushing your cat's teeth to stick to *gentle* brushing, as with red to white brushing for human beings – only use very soft toothbrushes with a small head, and a toothpaste suitable for cats. In most cats the inner face of the teeth will be inaccessible, but this area, by contrast with human beings, is not so susceptible to tartar buildup. Following the brushing of the teeth, cats of course deserve to be given a treat as a reward.

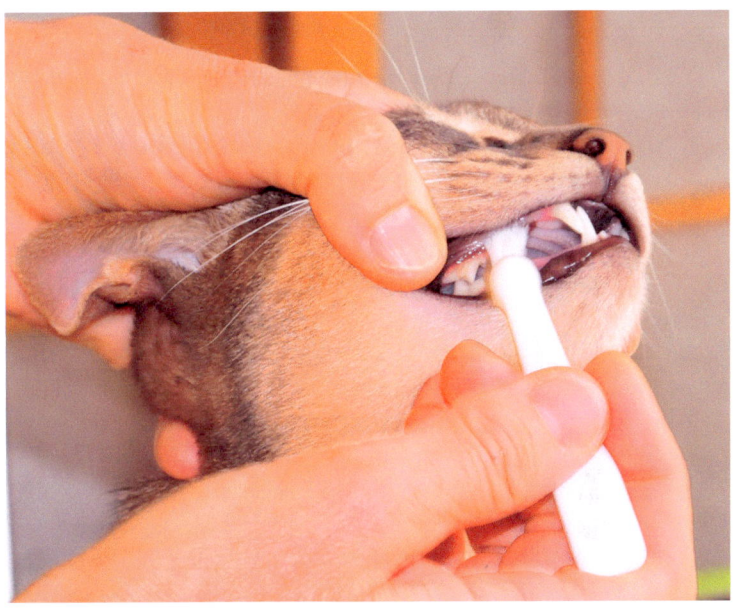

Skyboy having his regular tooth brushing routine – when you learn this at an early stage, it becomes an established part of a cat's life.

Bathing

For most cats, bathing doesn't really come into question – even if they like playing with water, that is quite a different thing from getting wet all over. Cats can swim, but they don't like it very much, because they cool off rapidly and their fur offers no insulation when wet. All the same, in later life it may prove necessary to give your cat a full or partial bath, for example if it has diarrhoea or has got dirty for other reasons.

For most young cats bathing is not the greatest experience of all time, but they can accept it in their horizon of experience with much less complaint as being just something that can happen. And incidentally it does often happen without being intended, when a young cat spends too long balancing on the edge of the bath tub!

The supreme principle with all educational exercises is not to subject the young cat to anything but the mildest stress, and on no account allow it to panic. So a bath needs to be given very carefully and slowly, with water at body temperature, and the cat needs to be reassured at all times that it can stand with its four paws on the base of the bath. Have a heated towel ready to dry the cat off when you have finished.

If you have the feeling that your young cat is unduly stressed by the bathing experience and may be losing its trust in you, you would be best advised not to force the issue.

Following a bath the young cat should be thoroughly rubbed dry, and then be given a warm place to look after its fur – which will keep it busy for the next hour. Although grooming will be the top priority for most young cats in this situation, all the same you can offer it a few very special treats by way of consolation.

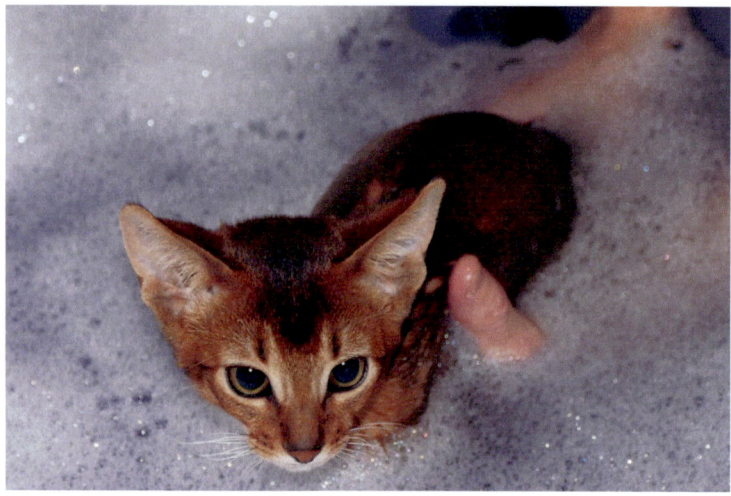

Bathing isn't something that causes Windy Whisper to break out in jubilation, but all the same it isn't the very worst life experience.

Learning words

Just like their names, *Sit* and *Come*, cats are of course capable of getting to know a whole lot of other words as well. The principle here is always the same: wait until the particular situation or action occurs, and when it happens, comment on it by using the word regularly.   After a few repetitions the cat learns that there must be a connection between the word and the given situation, it has succeeded in joining the dots.

Many cat owners already have a more or less intuitive awareness of this, and resort to it in relating to their pets, but the cat's capacity for developing a really extensive vocabulary continues to be much underestimated, and so is not really adequately exploited for the purposes of education and everyday communication.

In later life it can be very helpful if you can give your cat information, or perhaps even put it in the wish box in order to ask it to make a decision or express its wishes. In any case it does justice to the cat's cognitive capacity if you empower your cat in this way and help it to get a better understanding of unclear situations. In a recently published study horses were taught to communicate, by means of a symbol they had learned, whether they would rather have a blanket put on them or taken off, or have no change made to the present situation. So our domestic animals are not lacking in cognitive skills, only lacking a common language – if we give them the possibility of communicating their wishes, there is a whole lot of room for improving the quality of the relationship…

Here, by way of suggestion, is a list of examples of useful everyday words that a cat is capable of learning:

- *Food*, or whatever you want to say for a cat's meal time
- *Treat* or *Goody*
- *Water*
- *Get dressed* for putting on the harness and/or Thundershirt
- *Get undressed*, for taking it off again

- *Get in*, for getting in the transport box
- *Wait*, for sitting in the transport box or all other situations where the cat has to cope with frustration, either expectantly or impatiently
- *Get out*, when the cat is allowed to get out of the transport box again
- *Home*, when the cat comes in from outside, or in combination, *Get in, home* when it gets into the transport box in a strange environment
- *Down*, for jumping down
- *Jump*, for jumping (up)
- *Out*, when you open a door for the cat, for example in the garden
- *Look out*, as an advance warning or notification about things that may cause anxiety, like loud and unpleasant noises – mixer, vacuum cleaner, drill
- *Play*, and of course too the names of the various toys
- *Run*, for cats who have a running wheel
- *Scratch*, when the cat makes scratch marks in the right place
- *Catch it*, as an invitation to catch something, e.g. a fly or fur mouse
- *Air raisin*, as a name for edible flying insects
- *Brush teeth*
- *Tablets*
- *Inhale*, for cats with asthma who need to inhale regularly
- *Keep still*, for confined sitting and all other manipulations where keeping still is required
- *Get in the box* for getting into the wish box
- *Go to your place* for sitting in a designated place
- *Lie down*, when you lay the cat down on its side or back
- *Brush* or *hairdo*, for brushing and grooming
- *Trim nails*
- Names of tricks
- Anything else you want to communicate to your cat by way of information, like the names of other cats, family members, places, situations etc.

Relaxing word

A quite specially valuable word should be reserved for the state of relaxed wellbeing, when the cat purrs contentedly, keeps its eyes half closed with pleasure, kneads a soft blanket with its paws and so on – whenever the cat is feeling good all round and enjoying life. Suitable here are words rarely used in an everyday context (including invented words or words in a foreign language), which can be drawn out in pronouncing them, like

- *schön (nice)* or *hyvää* (Finnish for good, pronounced *hüüwa*)

*The quintessence of pleasure for Skyboy – an ideal situation for associating a nice relaxing word like **schön** with this sense of feeling good.*

Based on classical conditioning, this word will be associated with the positive state of relaxation the cat is currently experiencing – and seeing that cats are incapable of autogenic training, this is a good way of reminding them of the pleasant state of relaxation in difficult situations or at times when they are wound up. So as not just to waste the desired effect on crisis situations, you should make a point of refreshing this relaxing word in appropriate feel-good situations the cat's whole life long.

Harness and leash

Tolerating a harness is something that kittens can learn, like all other exercises, relatively quickly and without difficulty – they are having new experiences every day, and in the first months of their lives they are still quite open-minded about adopting them in their repertoire of what forms part of a cat's life.

As with tooth brushing, you may think this kind of training, like walking on a leash, is absurd in the case of cats, or at least unnecessary. You don't have to take cats for walks – but you can do! And yet the harness and leash can be extremely useful in other situations as well, not just for going on walks. For example, when you want cats to get to know one another in more or less controlled conditions, without the risk of an attack. The life expectation of a cat today is already in many cases over 20 years, and we never know what can happen or what changes may occur in such a long cat's life, or indeed in our own.

And even if you never feel the urge to make little excursions with your cat, or feel the need of a harness and leash – in the last resort it is just one more experience which expands the horizon of a cat and makes it more flexible in other situations, because it is more experienced.

If you would like to make little on-the-spot walks or extensive walks with your cat, it makes sense to buy an anatomically suitable cat-friendly harness with an elastic leash right from the start. The *Come with me Kitty®* harness, developed by vets, has the crossed straps resting on the breastbone (where a bit of pressure will not be a problem), with a collar that runs along the side of the neck / in front of the shoulder and a chest strap with two clips on the sides. The essential thing is that the front neckband does not really rest on the neck and the windpipe, but stays to the side, so that even when you pull the leash, or if the cat suddenly jumps or runs off, it will never feel pressure on this sensitive area and so panic.

An elastic leash provides further cushioning for sudden pulls and jumps, and prevents injury occurring.

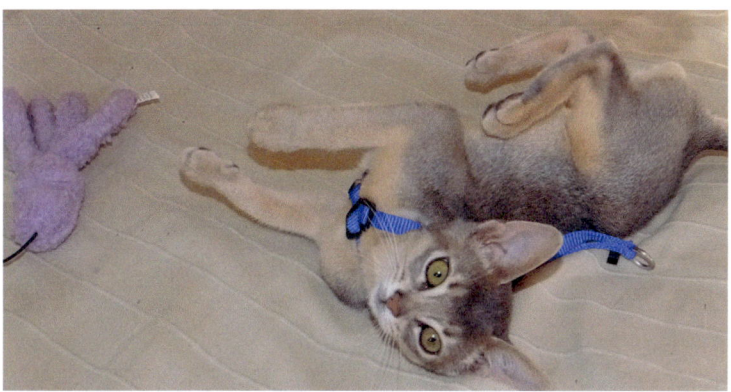

The first few times the harness makes Sunnyboy feel a bit uncomfortable, and he tries to get it off again.

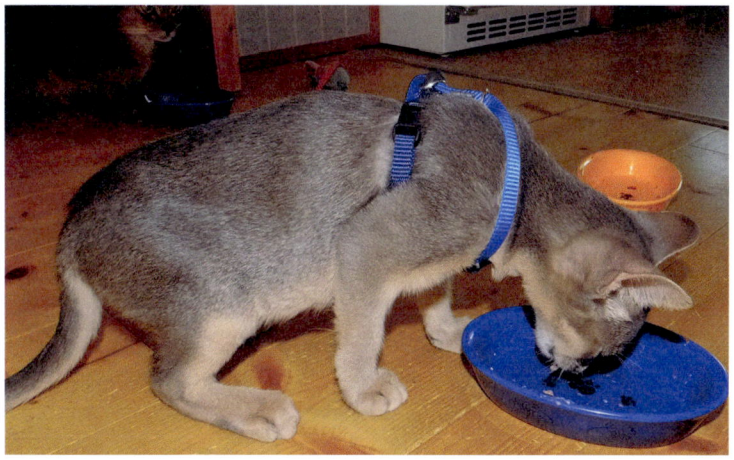

When you put on the harness before a tasty meal or a play session, wearing it soon becomes a habit.

The typical reaction of kittens who have a harness put on them for the first time is either to try somehow to get it off again, or else to freeze in complete immobility. This has to do with the new and unfamiliar physical sensation, and passes quickly, especially with young cats. The learning process of habituation will be facilitated and speeded up considerably if putting on and wearing the harness is combined with cheerful activities like playing or food.

So you notify the cat to *Get dressed* and show it the harness – you then give it a *click* and a treat for looking at, sniffing or playing with the little straps. After a few repetitions you carefully pull the neck strap over its head from the front; possibly the cat will put its own head through, if you hold it open and tempt it by holding out a treat. After a few repetitions with *Get dressed* and *Get undressed* comes the next step, with the closing of the chest strap. Depending on the cat's sensitivity, after a short pause for reflection one of the reactions mentioned earlier may occur – but these can easily be diverted into positive channels with a treat or an invitation to play. If your kitten shows extreme discomfort in the harness, or is so frightened that it is incapable of being distracted by pleasant things, take the harness off, leave it for a day and then start the habituation process again, much more slowly and in tiny steps with a lot of rewards along the way.

The average young cat will come to terms with the harness in just a few training sessions of 5 to 30 minutes duration, and will just take note of it as a normal part of its experience. Only when you have reached this point should you proceed to the next stage of using the leash for the first time, with the leash just dangling from the harness to begin with. When your kitten has taken note of this state of things, you can follow it around the apartment with the leash in your hand. Many cats find it somewhat irritating if you follow them every step of the way, and will need first to get used to being accompanied like this. Cats are not pulled on the leash, but always just called or invited – and for this you can use the nose target, the cat's name and the *Come* signal, or else you can get your young cat to come to you with food or a toy. If none of these ways work, it is better to pick up the kitten and carry it to the desired spot, rather than pulling on the leash!

Thundershirt®

Windy Whisper already wears the Thundershirt as a complete matter of course.

The Thundershirt® is a closely fitting body wrap, originally developed for dogs, with Velcro fastenings. The idea is that this narrow confinement of the body has a calming effect and reduces anxiety. Similar observations have been made with cats, who are less frightened on being transported and on visits to the vet – provided they have become habituated to it beforehand.

But cats will react at the beginning to any kind of 'clothing' – whether it is a harness, a Thundershirt®, a bandage or a dressing on the paw – with resistance or by freezing completely. A great many cats just fall over like a log when they wear a Thundershirt® for the first time, because they can't cope with this unfamiliar alien sensation of having their body constricted. But young cats can learn how to deal with this new physical sensation in a very short time – especially if you support the learning process with interactive play.

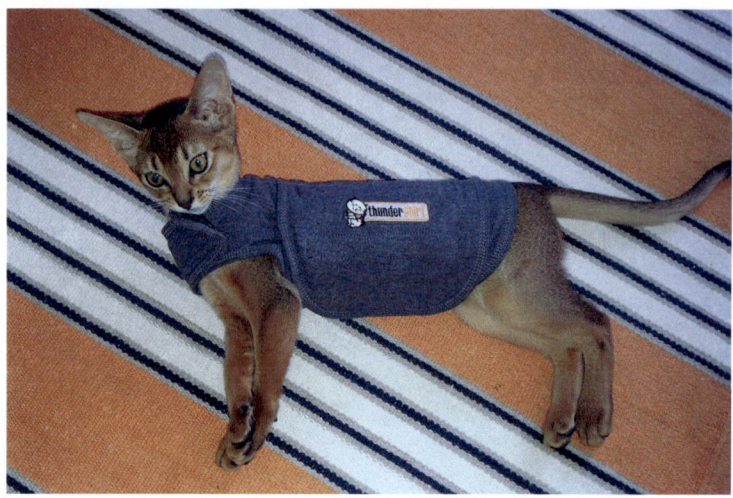

A typical first reaction to the new physical sensation – Fiji File falls over like a log.

Even when well habituated, most cats will still experience certain inhibitions and be a little subdued – they can no longer turn around if they fall, and with the shoulder blades restricted they are no longer so agile to jump and climb – but there are times when this is actually useful from an educational point of view. Above all hyper, hectic and very active cats will benefit from this simple measure, becoming in a way more centred and more aware of their own body, rather than dashing around without any inhibitions. After a first phase of habituation the Thundershirt® can even make a further contribution to relaxation, based on classical conditioning with the relaxation word the cat has learned together with appropriate happy and relaxing events.

Even if you have a superbly good, calm young cat who does not need to have set times imposed for self-reflection, practising with the Thundershirt® still makes sense. Like so many other things in a cat's life with which it is unclear whether they are later going to be needed or not, it is just an experience, a new sensory stimulus for the sense of touch and self-awareness. An experience similar to the Thundershirt® would be a bandage or body coat, for example, such as cats sometimes have to wear to protect wounds following an operation. Being reminded, in this kind of situation, of something familiar from childhood can at any rate reduce the psychological stress of a treatment.

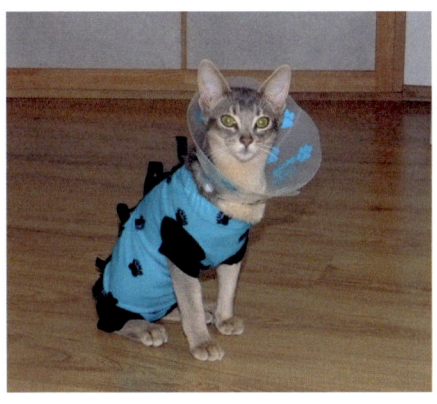

It could happen to any cat at some time in its life – a body coat and E-collar to protect wounds. Sunnyboy can hark back to this youthful experience at any time.

And if your cat is occasionally frightened when it reaches adulthood, then the familiar Thundershirt® can give it a feeling of security, and even relaxation, when it has to go to the vet.

Alternatively you can give the cat a similar experience with light whole-body wrap – for example with a silk scarf or tape – the important thing is that you keep an eye on your kitten when it is wearing a body wrap, to ensure that it doesn't get caught up or entangled accidentally.

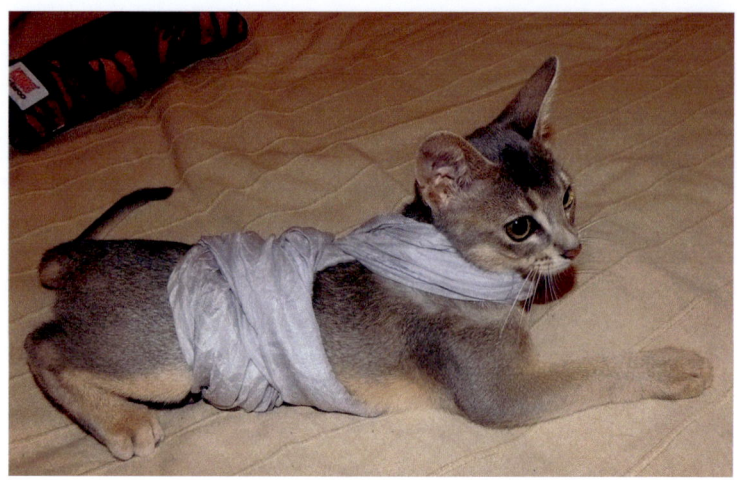

A light silk scarf as a body wrap, or elastic Vetrap tape, can also be used to give a young cat new physical sensations in a playful context.

Transport box

Starting box game

When you play this interactive learning game, your young cat will very soon be going into its transport box with highly positive expectations – because, you see, it is going to turn into the starting box for a game!

Horses and dogs have to go into a tight starting box before a race, emerging from it in order to race – and these sporty racers too have to learn to put up with the confinement of the box, and associate it positively with the start.

Put your frisky kitten in the transport box in a friendly way, preventing its escaping immediately with minimum effort. Usually it is enough to hold your outspread hand in front of the opening, or leave the door slightly ajar. The important thing is that the exit should quickly become free again when the starting signal is given. You let the kitten wait for one or two seconds, give a *click* and just at this moment let it start a game you have ready prepared – a feather teaser or a wand cat toy are the best for this, because you retain control. After 15-30 seconds you say *Get in* and put the kitten in the box again, *Wait* for a few seconds – then *click* and the supercool game resumes.

Skyboy waits excitedly as if in a starting box for the moment when he will be allowed to start the next game.

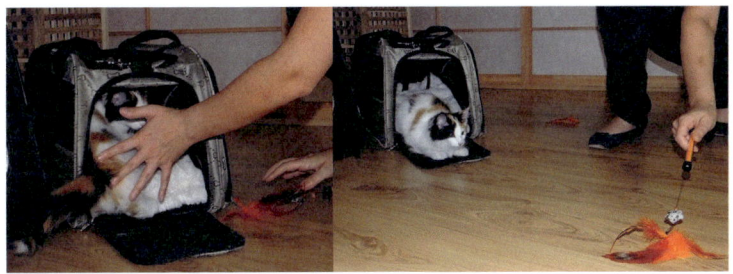

With Octavia it is enough to block the starting box symbolically with the hand, before she is allowed, after a short waiting time, to start playing with her feather teaser.

After just a few repetitions any resistance the kitten may feel to start with will have evaporated – it has grasped the sequence of the starting box game, and will get into the box in a mood of delighted anticipation, turn directly around and wait for the start. Now it is just a question of practice and daily repetitions, training the cat's patience with longer periods of waiting before the start. At some point your young cat will even decide, in the midst of its daily interactive play, to involve the transport box in the game of its own initiative and use it as cover.

A further extension of the starting box game is to offer the box with *Get in* in other places as well – when visiting strange apartments, in the garden or on outdoor excursions. Voluntarily getting into the box and waiting there thus becomes a normal, and even entertaining part of the cat's everyday routine. In crisis situations, when the cat is stressed or reacts with anxiety, the transport box can thus become a perfect signal of safety and protection, without your needing to touch or manipulate the cat in this exceptional situation – all you have to do is to offer the box and say *Get in*.

Get in *and* **Wait** *in the box – an extraordinarily useful exercise for lots of life situations.*

The transport box can also always be incorporated in an everyday context, as a place for quiet reflection and rest – as a temporary safety measure when you are tidying up, or when a cat at the age of puberty is getting quite out of control and tearing through the house without restraint.

> **But a stay in the box should always be followed by a positive happening, like a game, treats, cuddling, clicker training or just a normal meal. On the other hand you should never let the cat out of the box if it meows or behaves restlessly in other ways – you only earn the right to leave the box by patient, quiet *Waiting!***

In order to maintain this positive relationship to the transport box, it is important to be as careful as possible when making short car journeys or carrying the box. Just think what it feels like to be sitting in a small plastic box which functions like a sound box, without any kind of stability, while being subjected to sudden unpredictable changes of direction.

> **NB: you should carry your cat in its box as carefully as a raw, thin-shelled egg!**

Very young kittens rarely have a problem with car journeys. The older they become, the more likely they are to experience unpleasant sensations or even nausea when travelling by car, or on the other hand the lack of practice may make itself felt.

Cats with travel sickness may vomit, but do not always do so. Nausea is often to be seen just in the facial expression, an increased secretion of saliva or a pitiful meowing. If you have the slightest suspicion that your cat becomes nauseous when travelling, it is sensible to give it appropriate treatment whenever you plan to make a journey. Even if your cat only gives the impression of being uneasy or stressed by this unfamiliar form of locomotion, it is just as well to give it a few treatments (e.g. with Zylkene®), otherwise the cat may form irreversibly negative associations.

Controlled play

In the development phase leading up to puberty, tom cats above all (but not exclusively male cats) have a tendency to play in a very wild, and indeed even brutal and uncontrolled manner. Rather than taking pleasure in this wild impetuosity and encouraging it, you should divert a game into more orderly channels when it seems to be getting out of control. Here the three target exercises are particularly useful – these can be incorporated in any game as simple rules for better impulse control.

The reward for the target exercise in this case will not be a *click* and food – the *click* will be followed by resumption of the game.

> **The important thing here is that during the break in the game for target practice, when you are waiting for the cat to touch your finger with its nose, your palm with its paw or to get into the wish box, the cat should not have access to the present toy or any other one – so they had better be removed from its field of vision completely.**
> **The simple rule for the cat is as follows:** *Just put 1 Euro in the machine with your target exercise, and then the game can go on immediately!*

You can expect to see a lack of cooperation, and independent efforts to resolve the situation, on the part of your intelligent young cat, who does not understand to begin with why it should accept this unnecessary interruption. With a bit of consistency, however, it will finally grasp the rule, after which cooperation can be taken for granted.

> **NB: try to find a good mean between controlled play and fun! The goal of the target exercises is not to spoil the fun of the game, but just, in an extreme case scenario, to encourage the cat's self-control and cooperation.**

*Simple target exercises – Sunnyboy in the **Sit** target – give the wild game meaningful rules, and from time to time foster self-control.*

Tricks

The educational approach outlined in this book is not so much concerned with teaching the cat tricks, but rather focuses on the essential *life skills* which make cats' cohabitation with human beings easier. But of course it is fun, and can add variety to the everyday life of the cat right into old age, if you also teach your active animal a few new tricks from time to time.

The learning principles always remain the same, whether you are teaching the cat to sit in the wish box, have its teeth cleaned or Sit Pretty. With the three basic target exercises described above, it is a simple matter to develop a few tricks. Particularly suitable in this context is the nose target exercise, because it can be used as a directional guide and pointer.

As a result of its basic education your cat has acquired the principle of learning from you, and all that you would still like teach it will only be limited by your creativity and by the motivation, individual talents and physical capacity of the cat.

Tricks are not necessary, but they are an entertaining enrichment of the cat's everyday routine: Sunnyboy lets himself be induced to Sit Pretty with the help of the nose target.

One of the simplest tricks is Sit Pretty – a well controlled sitting on the back legs – just the way meerkats do it. When your cat is already well familiar with the nose target and responds to it correctly, just place your finger a little way above its nose so that it will have to stretch out a little bit. In quite small steps you can now draw the cat upward, until its front legs are off the floor and it is sitting on its hind legs. It is important here to proceed slowly, otherwise there is a risk that your kitten will jump up and reach for the target with its forepaws, rather than lifting itself up in a slow and controlled way.

Other ideas and suggestions for numerous other tricks like the roll, the slalom, *high five* and many more may be found in the appropriate books and DVDs – but this would be to go beyond the limits of the basic education for cats that we are concerned with here.

Having experiences

For kittens, every day is full of new adventures and experiences – it is all new to them. From the time they open their eyes at about one week of age until puberty at around six months, healthy young cats are open, inquisitive and playful in relation to practically all new experiences. They continuously learn from everything they encounter something for life. But the time is short, and at latest from puberty or the age of young adulthood, and sometimes even earlier, this carefree attitude gives way to a certain caution, restraint and even mistrust in relation to what is new and unfamiliar.

But the bigger the database of experiences accumulated by the cat in the first half year of its life, the more relaxed it will be in dealing with new things, more or less based on the motto: *been there, done that – I know all about it.*

So feline education also means giving a young cat as many positive experiences as possible in this crucial phase of life – completely independently of whether or not you think it is going to have some relevance at a later stage. It is just a matter of giving the cat the widest possible horizons taken all in all – giving it experiences which it associates with delight, curiosity and other positive emotions.

An experience can in principle be anything that the cat can perceive with one of its senses, self-executed or passively experienced actions, adventures, interaction in the form of games or encounters with other creatures.

In a house – and even in the garden – there is far too little new information from an educational point of view, so that you will be particularly challenged in this respect in the first half year of your cat's life. But it will absolutely pay off if you invest time and energy in this area!

Depending on the intensity and the possibilities available, new experiences should be offered in the first 24 weeks from once a day up to every two weeks. Every sense should be stimulated by a new adventure at least once a week – with young cats this is easy enough, as for them everything is new!

All sensory perceptions – hearing, seeing, smell, taste and touch – can be trained either individually or combined into more complex experiences.

By way of illustration, here are a few examples of new experiences for the cat:

- New sounds: cats are basically very sensitive to noise, and normal speaking volume or room volume is already loud as far as they are concerned; sneezing, coughing and laughter are often too loud for them. It is all the more important to ensure that various new noises crop up in the course of everyday. This includes the environmental noise with which you have to reckon anyway, like garbage disposal, lawn mowers, noisy children, traffic and (depending on the season) fireworks and thunderstorms. But other special noises as well, such as crackling paper bags, hair dryers, bubble wrap, vacuum cleaners, mixing machines, drills, knocking and hammering and loud music, should be actively involved in the cat's education. Particularly unpleasant or loud noises can regularly be commented on with a word like *Look out*, so that you can use this as warning information in a situation where there is going to be unavoidable ambient noise. Special sound CDs are available, with which you can offer your cat noises that are not so easy to reproduce, like fireworks, thunder or the wind.

- New odours: cats have a much better sense of smell than we do, and odours are a very important part of their environment. New odours can used as a positive environmental variation and as a reward – for instance catnip, Japanese catnip (silvervine), valerian, olive oil (or olive wood) – but not all cats will find all odours pleasant. Intensive biological odours will cause many cats to get rid of them by burying them – this applies to excretions like faeces and urine, and equally to food with a penetrating odour, vinegar, beer and other foodstuffs. And last but not least all natural scents from outdoors, like fresh plants, moss, wood, feathers, fur, leather, organic eggs and paper bags (cut off the handles) or a new cardboard box, can contribute to variations of smells – in this area there are no bounds set to creativity.
- New tastes: cats have a strong tendency to specialise in one kind of taste, and may stubbornly refuse all other kinds of food once they have got into this mode. It is all the more important to offer them as many different kinds and types of food and as many different tastes as possible right from

the start. It is quite unimportant whether this is a special kitten food or not. Individual meals can contain food for adult cats without any problem – the most important thing is the experience of new tastes and variety. Many young cats are interested in every possible kind of foodstuff – top of the list, of course, are all kinds of dairy products, but they will certainly taste things like cake, biscuits, brioche, popcorn, various kinds of vegetable and of course also meat and sausage products. These human foods are not really suitable for the cat's daily diet, but in reasonable measure and when used strategically they can be a fabulous and highly motivating reward when training your cat. Fresh pieces of beef or even – if you can cope with it – deep-frozen one-day chickens or mice will enrich the experience of a young cat, and may even encourage a more varied menu subsequently.

Windy Whisper plays the wild animal: a piece of reindeer fur brings many new sensory experiences and variety into the life of a young cat.

- New surfaces: if the cat is exclusively restricted to laminated or carpet floors, its sense of touch remains largely unused. New substrata like gravel and sand floors, asphalt, lawns and meadows can easily be experienced on outdoor excursions. When indoors you can involve all kinds of substratum as part of a game – anything from fur to artificial grass doormats, from grid structures to bioplastic flakes, can be tried.
- New toys: as with food, cats often develop preferences for quite specific kinds of prey. When they are young, different varieties of game are not so important; but the more different kinds of prey the young cat gets to know, the easier it will be later on to incorporate plenty of variety in your play sessions. At least once a week you should introduce a new type of prey object – whether homemade or purchased is unimportant!

Bioplastic flakes immediately make the hunting game twice as exciting for Fiji File!

- New physical sensations: many of the things we expect of cats have never been included in their natural learning programme. These include bathing for example, wearing a harness with a leash and even wearing an E-collar. New textile materials in contact with their body, like a bandage, body wrap or Thundershirt, are likewise completely new experiences for them, and may in some cases be found irritating at first. Seeing that you can never predict, in the course of a cat's life, whether one of these things may be found necessary, it is worthwhile carefully familiarising your young cat with them from an early stage. Young cats will get used to this new physical sensation in a very short space of time – above all when you put it across in a positive way, in combination with a lively game or a tasty treat. Most of these exercises – with the exception of the harness and leash, and the Thundershirt – will only need to be practised once or twice. It is not a matter of generating stress for the cat, but rather of incorporating these things as part of its horizon of experience, and showing it that they are not so bad after all.

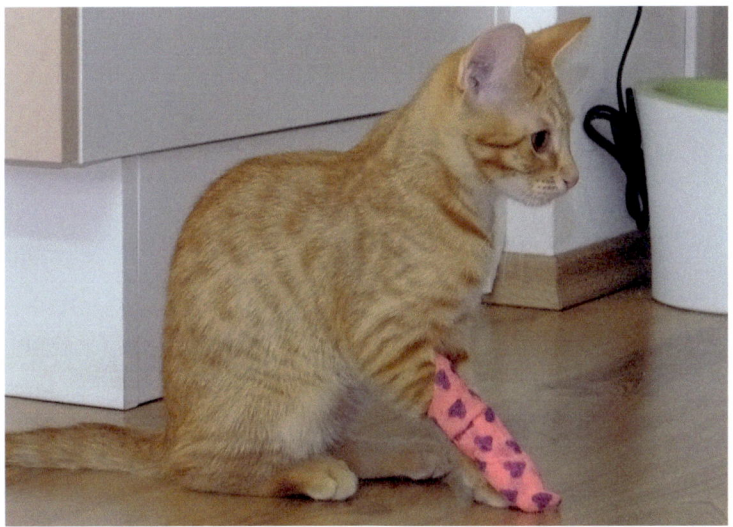

In the kitten kindergarten, Dexter wants to go on playing even with a bandage around his paw.

Sunnyboy learns how to eat with an E-collar early on – you never know what may happen!

Meeting his own reflection in the mirror – another new experience for Sunnyboy.

- New acquaintances: the cat's horizon also includes its social environment, and getting to know other creatures can definitely be an enriching experience. People strike us as quite obviously all belonging to the human race – but for a cat it is not so obvious that infants, squealing small children, schoolchildren and adult men and women are all members of the same species. So it is important to introduce a young cat to as many sub-groups of the human species as possible in emotionally positive situations.

And other animal species as well expand the cat's horizon – along with dogs, this includes small animals like guinea pigs and rabbits; all kinds of poultry, like chickens, ducks and geese; farm animals from sheep and goats to horses, and wild animals like hedgehogs. Some of these encounters will be exciting, or perhaps even appeal to the cat's hunting interest; large animals may however be perceived as threatening. None of these encounters should induce fear in the cat, or (vice versa) represent a threat to another animal – and the transport box should always be near at hand, as a safe place to retreat to.

Encounters with other domestic animals make for exciting variety on short excursions: Fiji File considers how to marshal the chickens, and Windy Whisper makes the acquaintance of a goat.

- New places: cats are creatures of habit, and leaving their familiar structures often disturbs or frightens them when they are adult. This makes it all the more important to teach them in the first few months of life how they can quickly find their feet in strange environments, by relying on additional reference points like the transport box, predictable rituals and their human being. You should take your young cat to a new location about once a week – the vet clinic, an office, houses of friends and relatives. NB: do make sure that these premises are safe and that your cat isn't going to get lost, fall from a window or balcony or be terrified by the sudden appearance of dogs or children. Visits to new places are also a perfect opportunity for practising little training routines like *Come*, coming to your whistle or *Kitty-kat say meow!*

Close encounters of a different kind:
kitten Sunnyboy meets a baby hedgehog in the garden.

Competence in solving problems

The supreme goal of early learning and education should be to give the cat the possibility of developing its own problem-solving abilities, if necessary also in cooperation with us human beings. The cognitive interaction of recognising a situation correctly, analysing it, making a decision and acting appropriately is the quintessence of intelligence – and for cats who live together with human beings the ability to ask for help, information and support would also be an extremely desirable faculty.

Here we are not of course concerned with mathematical or philosophical questions, but with daily problems which may crop up in the life of a cat, with or without human beings.

But giving further encouragement and stimulus to the cat's already well developed intelligence can be a very sharp two-edged sword! This is because what cats know and learn to do will be used by them to their own advantage – whether we like it or not. Cognitive capacity also includes the ability of applying a solution that is already known to a different, similar problem and making individual adjustments. So it can happen that the development of a cat's intelligence presents major challenges, because the cat starts to find its own solutions. At the same time, however, education and communication do also give rise to a new kind of relationship, based on which it is easier to tell the cat what you want and what you don't want.

There are few specific exercises for training the cat's competence to problem-solving – some situations just arise in an everyday situation, and you have to make use of them as they occur. If a young cat has been successful in finding a solution or way around a problem, it may voluntarily get itself into the same situation a few more times, because plainly it enjoys the repeated experience of success.

A few simple problem situations can however be set up deliberately and practised:

Opening doors

Simple problem solution: Sunnyboy learns how to push against a door and open it when it is ajar.

A problem that is simple enough on the face of it, which however surprisingly not all cats learn to resolve, is how to open a door, by pushing or pulling, when it is *ajar*. The more straightforward part of the exercise is pushing the door away from oneself, using the head or whole body – the more challenging second part is pulling the door towards oneself with the paw. For lively cats it can be a case of seeing the problem and solving it instantly, but for less determined young cats the situation may appear quite irresoluble at first glance.

The exercise becomes easier if the cat's motivation to get to the other side is heightened by your calling and offering food, or if the crack is so wide that the cat can almost get through already. Once the principle has been grasped, the other direction will usually work as well.

> NB: it is inadvisable to show your cat how it can actually open a closed door – intelligent and motivated cats are all too good at learning how to do it on their own account, just by observing their human beings.

Cat door

If you want your cat to be able to use a cat door later on, so it can come and go independently, or so that you can make some indoor rooms selectively accessible, a small exercise session will be found useful. If your cat flap has not yet been installed, then you can incorporate it in a game in any way you like. If it is already installed, you can also make a small replica in cardboard to illustrate the principle of going through it. With a transparent piece of foil or a towel, you can also practise overcoming the resistance of the flap.

> NB: if when you are practising you open the flap or hold it open for the cat, this should always be in the right direction – the way the cat would open the flap for itself. If you open the flap the wrong way and then let go of it too early by mistake, the cat's tail will be painfully

pinched and the flap pulled still tighter shut when the cat tries to escape.

Have regard to the lighting on the approaches to the cat door on both sides – you need a secure access and on the exterior some kind of cover, so that the cat will not immediately be exposed on a big wide space in the open air.

Kitty-kat say meow!

With this exercise we are concerned to teach the cat how to let us know it has a problem when it has been accidentally shut in somewhere. The proverbial curiosity of cats often results in their being shut in – if they are roaming cats in strange garages, or in attics and cellars. But even in quite large apartments and houses there are places you would never dream of, when the cat goes missing – like a cupboard, laundry storage space or the crack behind the drawers that you can only get into when a drawer is open.

In all these situations it is extremely useful if the cat has learned to pipe up and respond, at least in answer to your call. For a very talkative cat this is hardly going to be a problem – but there really are some cats who get shut into places like this for days at a time, without uttering a squeak in this unfortunate situation.

This exercise should be practised preferably in strange apartments, and not too intensively on your own premises. The cat should not be allowed to get the wrong impression and think it will always be let out when it meows. For the same reason, you should never use the transport box for this purpose!

Once the cat knows its own name, and will actually come when you call *Come* or whistle for it, you can try out this exercise when visiting a strange apartment. You shut up the cat 'by accident' in a small store room, box or drawer offering sufficient space, and wait, depending on how exciting the place is, for a few minutes. If the cat knows that you are in any case aware that it is shut in, it may not say anything. If it meows without being prompted, you call to it and invite it to signal again, then let it out immediately. If it keeps quiet, you wait a bit longer and go on calling until a clear response comes back. The cat needs to learn that it absolutely has to send a signal if it wants to be let out again. Occasional repetitions every few months make sense, especially for free-roaming cats.

> **NB:** on no account should you practise this exercise with the transport box, or with a familiar room in your own apartment, where you may want to sequestrate the cat temporarily. Ideally the cat should not associate the exercise with places where we might need to confine it at certain periods.

Burrowing game

The burrowing game is one of those exercises that are easy to organise. The first, very simple part consists in just laying a big blanket over the kitten and letting it look for a way out. At the next level you can create a mild stress situation by making the exit more difficult to find, because the blanket or fitted sheet is closed along all the edges apart from a small opening that has been left clear. Alternatively a quilt cover is also suitable – cats like getting lost in these. The goal of this exercise is to teach the young cat, in what appears to be a situation without any exit, to look for the way out in a systematic and oriented way, without getting over-excited. The thing here is the experience of a mild stress situation, and the feeling of success and self-confidence which results from the cat's finding its own solution to the problem.

> **NB:** the stress of being trapped should really only be mild, and not make the kitten anxious! This exercise commonly

develops into a delightful game, so every time you make the bed becomes an entertainment.

Sitting under a box

Another task where the cat liberates itself from an awkward situation. Place a cardboard box over the cat – the box should not be too big, the cat must be able to lift or push it around. Most young cats will slide around with the box, stick out their paws and perhaps even meow. Give the cat time to solve the problem and help it a bit, by lifting the box just slightly, if it sounds too desperate. In the long term this situation as well can be incorporated in interactive play sessions.

Getting themselves out of tight corners or calling for help should form part of cats' problem-solving repertoire.

Going backwards

On the face of it not a particularly demanding task – but going backwards in a dead-end situation is still something that a young cat needs to have tried once. Narrow ledges, slats, tight cul de sacs and the like where the cat cannot turn round are suitable for this exercise. Once the cat has recognised its position and started slowly to teeter in reverse direction, you give it your acknowledgement and supply a word, like *Backwards*, for this action.

Sunnyboy in a dead end: going backwards is not really difficult for a cat, but they need to have learned how to do it all the same.

Climbing backwards

Many fire brigade callouts would be unnecessary if cats had learned when they were young how to climb down a tree backwards. Evidently this is not an obvious solution for all cats, and it is one of the life lessons that they learn from their mothers by observation. When they are not too far off the ground they can jump down directly, but if it is a great height, many cats will lack the courage and freeze, unable to go either forwards or backwards. Planned exercises to encourage backwards climbing should rule out the possibility of a direct jump, so that the cat can really only get back by climbing down in the same way as it climbed up previously. As most climbing trees have enough intermediate steps, an indoor setting hardly offers situations where it is possible or necessary to climb backwards. For cats who are sometime going to be allowed out into the great outdoors, outdoor excursions are a suitable option, where the cat can practise its climbing skills, while secured on an elastic leash, on trees within human reach. Once it has learned how to do it, it probably won't need any further exercises for this faculty.

Overcoming obstacles on a walk – cats live intensively with the third dimension.

Jumping on your back or shoulders

This again is an exercise which, while extremely useful, does also come with a certain risk. Most cats see human shoulders or backs as a base too insecure to be used as an intermediate stop when they are sitting at a great height. But if a cat has learned in its youth that it can place its trust in this springboard, it is easy to rescue the cat from a great altitude if no other intermediate jumps present themselves. The important thing here is to do the exercise only in response to a direct invitation, to prevent the cat's coming to see human beings as such as a new kind of playground – never mind whether they are dressed or not, and whether they are prepared or otherwise.

Place your kitten on a table at a height from which it doesn't yet dare to jump directly to the floor. Offer your back as an intermediate step, by getting down on all fours and inviting the cat with a toy, food and an encouraging *Hop!* to jump. After a few repetitions this becomes a fun game which the cat is happy to join in. Another possible way of getting cats familiar with the human back is to use it as a beast of burden as part of your game, and get the cat to ride on it.

In individual everyday situations with a young cat you can find countless possibilities of presenting it with tasks where a solution is possible:

- Getting out of the dry (and later out of the wet and slippery) bath tub
- Stepping onto the greaseproof paper or yogurt lid, instead of pushing it around
- Choosing a different path when the direct one is blocked or inaccessible
- Finding access to a hidden food
- Finding the way down from a high spot.

Whenever an everyday problem crops up, accept the invitation and give your cat time to resolve the problem.

The nose target can of course always be used as an additional resource or pointer; and patience, confirmation when the cat makes the right move and positive feedback will encourage the cat's problem-solving ability. Along with the successful feeling of having found the solution, cats are really happy with acknowledgement and a relaxing reward in the form of treats or a game. And there are even some cats who will get into the same situation again voluntarily, in order to try out the solution yet again!

But these situations should never go beyond the experience of mild stress – encouraging the search for a solution. Significant stress, anxiety or desperation will block any kind of learning, and in the worst case scenario can have a negative effect on other learning situations you set up, because the cat no longer trusts you.

What about things that aren't allowed?

Not-doing – or how to keep a cat from doing something you don't want it to – remains the most frequent query in relation to feline education. Even when the principle of positive reinforcement has apparently been understood in theory, this question nonetheless keeps cropping up as long as there is a want of real practice.

You see, the idea and the intention of all the approaches outlined above is to prevent this problem's occurring altogether – or swiftly create a diversion into desirable channels with the help of guided educational resources.

Scratching and biting are among the common problems, or rather misunderstandings, with young cats. What looks like naughtiness – and does actually hurt – is usually perfectly normal behaviour on the part of a young cat, and is not uncommonly attributable to human educational error. To begin with, not all kittens have been given an equally good basic education by their mothers, or in the worst case they may even have been hand reared. Rough behaviour when playing, with scratching and biting, is however very often positively encouraged by animated movements of the hands. Depending on the degree of self-control that has been reached, an invitation to play with the fingers can escalate into a violent and brutal fighting game, above all with young cats close to puberty.

 Fingers, hands, feet and toes will be used by young cats in need of stimulus, and either intensively hunted as prey or treated as wrestling partners for a fighting game – both of these are notably unpleasant and painful, and will seriously affect your relationship with your cat! If you let this behaviour become ingrained in the first few months – as it is after all amusing, and doesn't hurt all that much as yet – unpredictable roughness will become an established character trait of the adult cat.

- First basic rule: hands, fingers and toes should never be offered as a plaything – this is to give the cat permission to hunt, bite and 'kill' them. Based on this misunderstanding, your hands will be bitten or scratched even when you try to pet your cat.
- Second basic rule: all playful hunting and fighting activities must be systematically diverted onto appropriate prey toys, and so kept in acceptable channels. Prey toys should be on long strings or wands, at any rate sufficiently far away from hands and feet to keep them out of the danger zone of an active young cat.
- If young cats bite and scratch when you pet them, it may be just the wrong time – and it is better at this moment to give them a wrestling toy or a stuffed animal as something to tussle with. On the other hand, young cats approaching puberty are quite capable of defending themselves roughly against petting, which may be perceived by them as rudely intrusive.

A further common problem, seen as naughtiness, is when cats climb up your trouser leg – or your naked leg, for that matter. Although most cats will automatically lose the habit from a certain age and as their weight increases, it is still unpleasant; and just waiting for it to go away may encourage this undesirable behaviour to become a habit. As when dogs jump up, cats' climbing on human beings is generally motivated by the desire to get a bit closer to us… or to anything else that may be found at a higher level, like food for instance. It just is natural to a kitten to look for a way up, and if a trouser leg offers itself as a climbing tree, then why not?

Here the basic solution, as with most other problems, is to recognise the cat's motivation, offer an alternative possibility, live out the behaviour in an acceptable spot and restrict positive feedback or the experience of success to this situation exclusively. In concrete terms this means rewarding your young cat quite consistently for sitting, and lifting it up frequently, when it has been sitting nicely, and placing it in a higher position – from where it has greater possibility of contact and also a good place for observation.

Notwithstanding, it can be useful at least to have a small tool of correction to hand – for those rare cases where you are in a great hurry, where it is crucial from the point of view of health and safety or if the cat really has an exorbitant nature and is determined to test all boundaries as thoroughly as possible.

Cats can actually take effective note of rules when they have been laid down consistently right from the start – for example, that certain doors, rooms or places are out of bounds. But the more experience of them the cat has already managed to acquire, the more difficult it will be to convince it of the contrary later on. If you start off by letting a young cat into the bedroom, at least occasionally, and then decide after six months that you don't want this anymore, you may well have set yourself up for an educational failure.

So ideally speaking, *no* always means *no* – right from the first day!

Even if it looks as if the cat is being markedly refractory or even stupid, because it just doesn't want to grasp the meaning of a prohibition – rest assured that neither the one nor the other is the case!

> **There is a great temptation to become more definite and to increase the pressure on the kitten, introducing stricter disciplinary measures or punishments. It may perhaps look as if this approach has been successful – but only at the high price of a damaged relationship!**

One of the goals of feline education is to create a trusting and affectionate relationship with the cat; and improbable as it may seem, when you have to do with a boisterous young cat – such a relationship is marked by mutuality, whereby the one can *say* to the other when there is something they don't like. You see, if your communication is basically characterised by a mood of positive friendliness, then in many cases it will be enough merely to hint at your disapprobation, by giving it vocal and emotional expression. A shake of the head, backed up by the unambiguous notification (which doesn't have to be loud) that there is something you just don't want to happen, will be registered and understood by your cat.

Mine!

The first simple exercise is something every small kitten who has grown up with its mother or siblings is already aware of. This is respect for the prey of another, and cats insist on this respect being shown with a very low-pitched grumbling growl. Above all kittens, but some adult cats as well, can be transformed at a stroke into terrifying wild animals when they have fresh meat, a mouse or a bird, or possibly even a toy mouse they are particularly fond of, between their teeth. They will defend their prized possession against all comers, by turning away, growling and (when absolutely necessary) with claws; and no other cat would ever dream of contesting the point. Only when the prey, in the course of play, has left the cat's personal zone is there the possibility of a change of ownership.

It is interesting that young cats understand and respect this *It's mine* or just *Mine!* message not only from other cats, but also when it comes from human beings. All you need to do, actually, is to say *Mine!* in a very definite way, in a slightly grumbling or minatory undertone – and it is most important that you should really mean it! The warning doesn't necessarily have to be loud, because it is intended to convey information, not to frighten the kitten. In case of need, and in connection with very attractive objects like ham for instance, you may have to be prepared at the beginning to block access with your hands and to repeat the message a number of times over – *That* belongs to *me*!

Mine, mine, all mine! Windy Whisper knows very well how to defend his prey, as well as respecting the prey of others.

Leave it!

This word of correction is a small emergency brake, but you should avoid using it too frequently in the course of the day for all kinds of trivialities, otherwise the meaningfulness and effect of it will be watered down by irrelevance. For the same reason it is better not to resort to a much too frequently and carelessly used *No*, but rather to use a short phrase like *Leave it, Forget it* or *Don't do it*.

This formulation, which is not entirely standard in a context of everyday speech, will be linked in training with an emotion of frustration and failure. The cat learns as a result that it is a complete waste of time to go on trying when it hears these words, because there is absolutely no chance of succeeding – so it will leave off at once.

The exercise is structured as follows:

- Sit or kneel in a relaxed way on the floor, and give your cat some quite small treats, in order to create an attitude of positive expectation.
- If your cat wants more, put a small piece in front of it, say calmly *Leave it* or *Don't do it*, and make **absolutely certain** that it is out of reach, by placing your hand over it or later, if you are standing up, treading on it and so ensuring that the cat is not going to get at it under any circumstances whatever.
- At the moment when the cat turns aside and no longer tries to get at the inaccessible treat, you make an immediate *click* (optional) and then give it, a little to one side, a **different** bit to reward it for compliance.
- After a few repetitions your cat should turn away immediately when it hears *Leave it*, without being bothered at all by the food which is in any case out of reach.
- With increasing confidence on your side, you can raise the level of difficulty by leaving the piece of food clearly visible – but you continue to watch over it from a safe distance like Cerberus, to make sure that the cat will **never** be allowed to get at this treat. But be warned – cats are very fast, and are good at advance planning!
- In subsequent steps of the exercise, you can quietly increase the distance or practise *Leave it* in a different context – e.g. with a toy, or other not unduly enticing situations.
- Keep the individual practice sessions short – five to ten repetitions are enough – in order to avoid creating a negative mood.

The big challenge here is the independence of the cat, who may put a great deal of effort into resolving this problem of the inaccessible food on its own account in some kind of creative way.

So it is advisable only to start this exercise once you have already got through several successful weeks of training with your cat. Then your cat will have learned first of all how to learn from you, in the best case it will even ask you for information when something is unclear, and it will above all have developed a certain amount of trust, so as to be able to handle the frustration you are going to cause it.

Negative conditioning

Strictly speaking it shouldn't be at all necessary, after the educational process outlined so far, to introduce any other negative measures. All forms of negative conditioning are very risky, because you cannot really predict all the associations the cat is likely to make in the circumstances.

Here's an example:
Your inexperienced young cat is playing with a wasp at the window. You speak to it sharply and make a swift movement to hold it back – and just at this moment it gets stung in the paw! There are many factors which the cat may associate negatively with the pain in this situation: *Wasps are unpleasant*, would be a reasonable and logical conclusion from the learning process!

But your cat may acquire a whole lot more convictions, or superstitions:

- All insects (including flies, butterflies, moths and midges) are dangerous
- The window is dangerous
- The person standing by – you – is dangerous
- Loud words are dangerous
- Rapid movements are dangerous
- …

This risk of encouraging fear that will be extrapolated to other similar situations is unfortunately par for the course with all negative experiences – which is why these strategies should be applied only with great caution and in a well considered way. *Don't you dare!*

One possibility of establishing a moderate negative conditioning, in a form the cat will understand, is to snap your finger on its ear. Adult cats who are friends, when they want to indicate their displeasure, sometimes snap and bite each other's ears without doing any real damage. Particularly stubborn and self-confident young cats, who really want to test the extreme limits with everything, can have a boundary established if you snap your finger on their ear from behind, combined with a softly minatory growling *Don't you dare.*

This negative conditioning should only be carried out **twice at most** – when it is correctly applied, actually just once will be enough. Wait till a situation arises where your young cat is sticking its nose in where it is not wanted – your ham sandwich, or the feeding bowl of another cat – position yourself behind the cat, and give a controlled snap of your finger on its ear from behind, while you say *Don't you dare.* In future just saying *Don't you dare* will be enough on its own to put the cat in mind of what you did to its ear.

> **NB: this negative conditioning should really be used extremely sparingly,** with self-confident young cats, in situations the cat finds easy to understand and only **always in combination** with immediate positive feedback, for example a nose target, an invitation to get in the wish box or the like.

Electric fence

The fence is not yet charged, but Sunnyboy will soon learn that the electric fence is a boundary that it is better not to touch.

Securing your garden with an electric fence is a form of negative conditioning where you accept the lesser risk of the cat's forming mistaken associations because the long-term benefits to the cat bulk larger.

Electric shocks have a notorious bad reputation in training generally, and many cat owners feel they are inhumane. By contrast with banned electric dog collars, electric fences are allowed as enclosures for all kinds of animals. The important difference is that the cat can see the fence, and decide just how much berth to give it – it's the cat's choice!

As the sole or additional means of securing your garden, an electric fence is a very simple, cheap and above all safe solution if you want to let your cat go out without any worries. As always, of course, there will be some extraordinary talented cats who will be sure to find an exit...

You can test the intensity of the electric shock for yourself – as you will see, it is an unpleasant but by no means dramatic experience, which is very likely to happen to you in your garden more frequently than it happens to your cat!

The important thing is that when the cat touches the wire it should be in contact with the ground – be earthed, in other words – as otherwise it will be unaffected by the current like a bird.

In order to reduce the risk of false associations being formed, you should be aware of a few things when securing your garden with an electric fence:

- Young cats should already be familiar with the garden, capable of moving around, playing and exploring outdoors under supervision in a spirit of trust and confidence. Ideally you should not switch on the electric fence when the cat is trying its first steps in the garden!
- Take care that the first garden excursion when the fence is switched on does not take place in wet conditions or after it has been raining, because this increases the conductivity.
- The escape route back indoors must be clear and unobstructed – the most likely reaction of the cat, after its first unpleasant contact with the fence, is to flee back into the house immediately, possibly even hiding in the remotest corner.

- Try to observe your young cat from a distance and without appearing involved – you don't want the cat to think it could have something to do with you.
- Depending on the cat's sensitivity, it may be minutes, hours or in some cases even days until the cat is brave enough to venture into the garden again. You should keep it company and encourage it to play.
- Cats learn very quickly to recognise the typical clicking of the rhythmic impulse of the leads through grasses and contact points, and above all to respect it.
- If in spite of everything your cat succeeds in finding a way out – this does happen occasionally – switch off the current at once, in order to make it easier for the cat to get home.

When it doesn't seem to be working

There will always be situations where it looks as if this approach to feline education is proving unsuccessful. But education always works, even if it may look like a failure at first glance. The reasons for lack of success when teaching cats are often simpler than you might think:

- Impatience: cats grasp things very quickly – most cats do – but they take their time before coming to a decision. If you are training a young cat for the first time in your life, the likelihood that you will be unduly impatient is extreme. Learning always involves a phase of latent learning – these are the intervening pauses in which the impressions and experiences come to be arranged and categorised in the brain. After some days, sometimes even weeks, flawless performance of the exercise will be completely taken for granted. Along with the apparent failure to grasp the meaning of an exercise, the phase of decision – which even a well educated cat is hardly going to be deprived of – can make it look as if things *aren't working*.

- The fabulous effects of education may then, in some cases, only really become apparent when the cat is adult – but they are then very persistent, and with a little repetition will be retained for the whole of the cat's life.
- Excessive expectations: along with impatience, too high expectations may cause obstacles in the cat's education, and the apparently minute progress being made, or even stagnation, can give the impression that it is all a failure. But don't forget that even if your young cat seems to be so independent, its development is not yet really complete. First comes kindergarten, then primary school, and only on this basis do you have further education leading eventually to university level – it is completely unrealistic to expect university standard performance from a kitten, when it has so much distraction in its life and so many new things to discover.
- Motivation problems: naturally speaking cats are not really team players, and have an innate tendency to try to look for a solution quite independently. All exercises that rely on the cat's cooperation will be decidedly rejected from time to time. It is obvious that the cat has understood what is expected of it, but it turns away and declines to cooperate. Either this is down to a temporary disinclination or tiredness on the cat's part, who after all is not so urgently in need of the thing it can have or wants; or you may have to do with a particularly stubborn or exceptionally intelligent cat, who is trying to take the direct route even on the basis of non-cooperation – more or less on the principle, *Why all these circuitous exercises, can't we just cut to the chase?* As a way out of this cul de sac, try better and more varied rewards, and more insistence on your side.
- The wrong plan: some failures are attributable to the fact that the emphasis has been placed on not-doing, on disciplinary rules, without at the same time showing or offering the cat any real alternative courses of action. An educational plan will always first of all entail the attempt to recognise the motivation of the cat, an at least equally attractive option for

channelling this activity and the consistent reward of desirable behaviour in the proper place.
- Bad experiences: eager to learn as young cats are, they can be equally sensitive to unpleasant or frightening experiences. Just a short moment that the kitten experiences as threatening can sensitise it in relation to all the conditions that are simultaneously present. If a noise frightens it or a manipulation is unduly prolonged, even the most fabulous reward isn't going to make a difference after that – the young cat will just continue to associate it all with the bad experience. The important thing, then, is to proceed with the cat's education very carefully, and to adapt your expectations to the individual cat's emotional resilience. In most cases these learning humps can be smoothed out again, but it calls for a great deal of sensitivity, creativity and patience.
- Sickness: although of course there are young cats who take a bit longer to grasp things or are not particularly motivated to learn something new, you should always take into account the possibility that the cat may be sick or feeling unwell. A fever, infections and even pains are stress factors which will demote the learning of new things to second or third place in the order of priorities.
- Anxiety: like physical illnesses, emotional problems – and above all anxiety – are a massive obstacle to learning. Young cats who are so anxious that they can't learn even the smallest exercise are definitely in need of therapeutic help.

Kitten kindergarten

The kitten kindergarten is an idea developed by the Australian behavioural therapist Kersti Seksel, with the idea of giving kittens, like puppies, a more thoroughgoing socialisation than has been the case in the past.

In Europe this idea has not yet really taken root – but we venture to hope and expect that in coming years the kitten kindergarten will become an increasingly familiar concept, partly thanks to this book.

The goal of the kitten kindergarten is first to give young cats a more or less formal framework for learning, usually in a veterinary practice committed to the project. By contrast with play groups for puppies, it is not so important for kittens to have social contact with one another and play together. It is more a matter of familiarising them with visits to the practice, the environment and the experience of being handled.

In addition, the kitten kindergarten aims to give you as a cat owner the possibility of finding out all kinds of new things about cats, with a view to prevent out any problems and misunderstandings in your shared life right from the start.

As it will probably be a few years before you are able to attend a proper formal kitten kindergarten with your kitten, in the meantime you can make use of this book.

You will find here a description of all the exercises and learning games currently suggested in my kitten kindergarten – making it effectively a complete manual for setting up your own kitten kindergarten at home. Nonetheless it is very important that you also involve your veterinary practice in the training – whether you need help with handling the kitten for a medical examination, or advice on a specific problem. Experience of the early training and education of cats is still relatively limited, and practically every kitten and its owner are going to come up with new ideas – or small mistakes are likely to be made, based on a lack of past experience.

So the kitten kindergarten is a concept still in the process of development, where cats are not the only learners…

Octavia and Sunnyboy playing together in the kitten kindergarden – a pleasant experience, but not an essential part of a cat's education.

Educating several cats

Cats are intrinsically social animals – even if they are still often seen as solitary individualists. Their solitary side shows itself, however, for the most part in connection with hunting activities. Above all for domestic cats who have very little variation in their lives, living with another cat can be a rewarding experience – assuming of course that the relationship is a good one and well balanced, and stays that way.

There is the best chance of this if you take on two kittens right from the start – ideally *of the same sex* – and let them grow up together. They may be siblings, but they can equally well be young cats from different litters. Up to puberty and into young adulthood, until approximately one year, affectionate friendships are still quite possible. The older the cats are when they get to know each other, the more challenging the encounter is likely to be and the chance of a deep friendship arising is less – although of course, given all the individuality of cats, you cannot ever rule it out completely.

The social nature of the cat is a big help for educational purposes, and at the same time it is a challenge.

Cats are notably social learners, above all in their early development – they observe another cat, and can adopt its modes of behaviour directly without further experiment. Some cats also learn by observation from human beings – for example, how to open doors, and sometimes even how to use the toilet.

So the education of a kitten becomes considerably simpler when you already have another cat in the house, who can function as a model and even sometimes play a directly active part in training. Some fine points of species-specific communication can actually only be learned from one cat to another. Cat mothers may even, in some cases, teach their kittens not to do certain things which they themselves have been warned to avoid.

So much for the benefit, but at the same time it can be a handicap. This is because young cats will absorb by observation absolutely *everything* in the way of undesirable behaviour, all the varieties of naughtiness and idiosyncrasy that have accumulated in the course of time and which will be passed on to the next generation like a tradition.

But even if it were only the good things that a young cat learns from a well educated adult cat – it learns all this quite independently of human beings. Of course other cats are in the nature of things more interesting and credible as teachers for a kitten. They belong to the same species, speak the same language and so have a decisive advantage over us humans.

You may think that learning is learning – does it matter how it happens? Well, yes and no – seeing that the small everyday exercises are particularly important for teaching a young cat the principle of learning from us human beings. When copied from another cat, the exercises will all function perfectly – but only when this cat is present, and not because we as humans are able to give the cat an individual invitation. It looks just as if the young cat simply adopts the actions without having any idea why – *If role model cat does it, I do it too, otherwise I don't have any reason to behave this way.* So the difference lies in the question from whom the cat has learned an exercise, and who it refers to in future in this connection.

Although this is not a major problem, and can be compensated for later on by more intensive individual training, it may nonetheless be advisable to schedule the occasional separate training session right from the start.

Two kittens of the same age are in any case going to distract each other such a lot as to rule out concentrated practice – at times their interest will be focused less on the human being than on their playing together. So in the early stages you should separate the kittens for a few minutes, above all when you start completely new exercises.

Once the young cats, after the first few repetitions, have understood the principle of the target exercises, there is of course no reason why you should not train them together – on the contrary. The *click* can perfectly well be the same sound for both cats. The additional information as to whose turn it is and to whom it applies can be supplied by calling the cat's name and turning in their direction, or by eye contact. If one of the two cats is given a passive exercise like *Sit in the box* or *Go to your place*, while the second is engaged with an active exercise (nose or paw target, manipulation or the like), the *click* and the reward will go to both simultaneously, seeing that both have done their exercise as expected. It can be very helpful to do the exercises not on the floor but on a table or chair, because it naturally delimits the space available for movement.

For your later life together, it makes a lot of sense if you have at least one perfectly ritualised exercise for the cats in your repertoire – *Sit on your place* or *Go to your places* – which is going to work quite automatically, quickly and without lengthy encouragement in all crisis situations. These team rituals give the cats security, especially in a social sense. If they are squabbling or stressed with one another, a ritual like this, which they can practise together, helps restore trust between them.

Last but not least, it is exceptionally exciting to observe how very greatly cats differ in their capacity for grasping things, their talents, their motivations and interests. In the course of their education you will get to know your cats better, and discover how different they are in their development.

*Educating more than one cat can be an exciting challenge, but it is quite easy to manage with the help of **Sit** targets.*

And how about older cats?

It goes without saying that adult cats, and even old cats, can perfectly well be trained. The educational techniques and principles all remain exactly the same. Never mind whether your cat is eight weeks or eight years old! So theoretically you could start this educational programme at any point in time.

At the same time, of course, there are going to be differences – and there are good reasons why this book is principally written with kittens in mind.

Young cats are still open in their development – without any past life experience, they could even be described as credulous. Without life experience and all the things they have already acquired in day to day living, it is a whole lot easier to convey to a cat that activities like grooming, brushing the teeth, wearing a harness with leash, sitting in the wish box or the transport box are the most normal thing imaginable in a cat's life. With a young cat you have a book of blank pages, in which you can inscribe a great many experiences from scratch – in the case of an adult cat you must look for space between the lines, in order to accommodate the new information you want to add. This is not completely impossible, but it is nothing like as quick and easy as with a kitten.

The longer a certain behaviour has established itself as a habit, the more difficult it becomes to change these habits – you will have to give your adult cat very convincing reasons to change its ways. If a cat can draw on a fund of life experience telling it that persistent meowing, scratching or other kinds of misbehaviour have sooner or later always yielded a successful result in the past, then you will need strong nerves at all events, and even more stringency, if you want to introduce new rules for success.

A good appetite, a liking for games and no undue mistrust of human beings will of course make it easier to educate an adult cat. It is certainly a major and a laborious task – but all the more rewarding – to teach an unsocialised or poorly socialised, traumatised cat some of the *life skills* which will however make their lives so much easier. If punishments are in any case a completely unsuitable tool in a cat's education, this applies all the more to the adult cat, who may start to defend itself or to withdraw, but in any case will cease to trust you.

Side-effects of education

Can the education of cats have side-effects? In a certain sense and seen from a certain standpoint, we might say Yes – seeing that the knowledge and experience you have conveyed to your cat are never going to be lost again. A wide-awake cat who has experienced and learned a great deal in its youth will remain more demanding its whole life long, and is unlikely to let itself be treated any longer as a couch potato, or left on the sidelines and ignored. It will steadily go on expanding its capacity for solving problems, and apply it to its own advantage. At the same time, intelligent lively cats are going to do that anyway – and with a solid education at least you can not only count on a much more affectionate relationship, based on understanding; you will also have more control and greater opportunity of communication! Experiencing and actually understanding cats, as emotional and cognitive beings, is such a very much more joyful experience that it won't feel like time or work invested, but more like just hanging out with a friend.

Life skills

Based on the idea and fabulous book of my two colleagues Helen Zulch and Daniel Mills, we can sum up all the educational themes for the cat which we have described here under the heading of *life skills*. These are all the capacities which make it easier for a cat to live with a human beings, and allow it to develop into an emotionally stable and flexible personality. *Life skills* are not orders and commands that cats are expected to obey, but rather communicative, cognitive and emotional capacities for dealing with practical everyday situations.

Cats are not miniature dogs, and education is not going to make them into dogs either. So the *life skills* important for kittens will be different from those of young dogs, in spite of a few overlaps. And it goes without saying that the skills listed below will again be different from what a free-roaming cat needs to know – one who lives more or less on its own resources, on the periphery of human society.

Here is a first attempt to draw up a list of indispensable *life skills for cats* who live with human beings:

- Learning from and with human beings, for better cooperation
- Expressing wishes and needs in such a way that they will be understood
- Getting into the transport box
- Taking tablets
- Accepting being handled, and simple manipulations like grooming and toothbrushing
- Tolerating medical examination by the vet
- Putting up with frustrations

- Curiosity and openness (possibly marked by caution) in relation to new things, situations and people
- Social skills in relating to other cats.

Training plan

This is the first attempt to draw up an educational programme of exercises and learning games, as comprehensively as possible, as a plan for your kitten up to the first year of its life. The following training plan should give you an overview of the training tasks you have to look forward to, and of when and how often it makes sense to carry them out. The recommendations for the frequency and intensity of the individual exercises have been based on practical experience from the last few years, and are not in any way scientifically proven.

> **Although the few weeks of speedy learning capability of a young cat really are very brief, the supreme principle remains that it must always be *relaxed* and *fun*. It would be the worst mistake you could make to overtax your young cat with misplaced ambition and too high expectations!**

The nice thing about educating a cat is that there is no kind of risk involved of turning it into a competition or some kind of superlative performance – because the moment this idea comes into your head, your cat will ensure that it turns out a resounding flop!

Please take the training plan, above all, as a suggestion, and by all means adapt it to your needs and necessities and those of your kitten. After one or two weeks most of the learning games and exercise will slot into your everyday routine quite automatically, so that the weekly or monthly plan will act more as a memo or pool of ideas.

The intensity and frequency of the different exercises is just intended as a guideline, above all to avoid putting too much pressure on your cat. As the cat becomes more experienced and more skilled, the exercises will generally be reduced quite automatically to occasional repetitions from once to three times a week to once a month.

With some exercises there will be an automatic overlap – for example, if you take your cat by car to a strange house, or for an outdoor excursion: get in the transport box, *Get dressed*, car trip, new environment, new substratum, new sounds, new smells, new encounters.

Exercises to be practised several times a day

Exercises that make sense when practised several times a day can practically always be organically integrated with your normal interaction as learning games for your kitten. Once to three times a day doesn't mean that all exercises absolutely must be carried out that frequently, but they can be.

- Formal clicker training with the three target exercises – nose, paw, sitting
- Informal clicker training, incorporating the target exercises, with which the kitten is by this time familiar, in everyday situations – before feeding, during games or in connection with anything the cat has set its heart on. Or just because you want to tell the kitten that it's doing something right – for example when using the scratching board, keeping still when you're examining its ears or because it's just sitting like a good cat.
- Interactive play with various prey toys in at least a weekly rhythm – changing to a new toy every week.

Daily exercises

- *Come* game, or coming when whistled for, followed by *Sit*
- Starting box game
- Toothbrushing as a gradually built up playful routine during the change of teeth, when the cat has its adult teeth then once a day
- One of the manipulation exercises, like confined sitting, grooming, touching paws, trimming nails, lying on the side, lying on the back
- Taking tablets – once a day with a maximum of three repetitions of one exercise; once the exercise is going well, reduce frequency to every one to three weeks
- *Leave it* game – only from four to five months, when formal and informal clicker training is working regularly and effectively; once a day repetition just until the exercise is going well, then reduce to every one to three weeks.

Exercises for practising once or twice a week

- Putting on the harness, and getting used to the leash
- Putting on Thundershirt®, body coat or T-shirt, or body wrap
- Sitting and waiting in the transport box with the door closed
- Visiting a strange house, office or the veterinary practice
- Outdoor excursions, once harness and leash are familiar
- Making a short car journey
- Experiencing something new – visit, dog, new food, new scent, new sound, new substratum
- Learning a new trick – if this interests you and your cat

One-off exercises

- Bathing
- Encounters with other animals (chickens, ducks, goats, sheep, horses)

User-friendly training plans which can be printed out in pdf format may be found on my website www.schroll.at under Katzen-Kindergarten [kitten kindergarten].

Passwords for opening the pdf files:

- Trainingsplan16
- Trainingsplan7

Afterword

Finally I would like to thank all kittens, along with their owners, who have given me so many suggestions, such a lot of feedback and pictures, and who have taken on board the idea of the kitten kindergarten as beta testers so enthusiastically and successfully.

Special thanks to my friend and colleague Hubert for his critical remarks and correction of the manuscript, his practical experience and photos.

And last but not least thanks to my partner Werner for the many pictures he provided, and for his quite special ability to sum things up with such cheerful conviction.

For my boygroup of cats Fiji File, Windy Whisper and Sunnyboy,

and of course
Skyboy.

Resources

- Mills D., Zulch H. Life Skills for Puppies. Laying the Foundation for a Loving, Lasting Relationship. Hubble & Hattie 2012
- Schroll S. Miez, Miez – na komm! [Puss, puss – come!] Books on Demand 2007.
- Laser B. Clickertraining – mehr als Spass für Katzen [Clicker training – more than just fun for cats]. 2012. www.lasercats.de
- Hauschild C. Tierarzttraining für Katzen: Einfühlsam und spielerisch zu mehr Gelassenheit [Veterinary training for cats: a sensitive and playful approach, for reduced stress]. Books on Demand 2014
- Dantas LMS., Delgado MM., Johnson I., Buffington CAT. Feeding puzzles for Cats. Feeding for Emotional and Physical Wellbeing. Journal of Feline Medicine and Surgery (2016) 18, 723–732. http://jfm.sagepub.com/content/18/9/723.full.pdf+html (08-10-16)
- Mejdell CM., Buvik T., Jørgensen GHM., Bøe KM. Horses can learn to use symbols to communicate their preferences. http://www.appliedanimalbehaviour.com/article/S0168-1591%2816%2930219-2/fulltext?rss=yes (08-10-16)
- Toxic plants database of the University of Zurich http://www.vetpharm.uzh.ch/reloader.htm?perldocs/links_g.htm?inhalt_c.htm

Index

A
Activity feeding
Administering tablets
Aggression, defensive

B
Bandage
Bath tub
Begging
Body coat

C
Calling, by name
Calling, with whistle
Cat flap
Cat food
Cat grass
Catnip
Cat's toys
Cat's toilet
Climbing
Clicker training
Clicker training, formal
Clicker training, informal
Grooming
Communication
Competence, problem-solving
Competence, social
Conditioning, instrumental
Conditioning, classical

D
Dining table

Drinking fountain . . . .

E
Educational assistant . . . .
Excursion . . . .
Electric fence . . . .

F
Feeding strategy . . . .
Food quantity . . . .
Foreign body . . . .
Freedom . . . .
Free roaming . . . .
Frustration, tolerance of . . . .

G
Games, interactive . . . .
Games, rough . . . .
Games, social . . . .
Garden . . . .

H
Hammock . . . .
Hiding places . . . .
Hopper window . . . .
House plants . . . .
Hot plate . . . .
Hunger . . . .
Hunting behaviour . . . .
Hunting games . . . .

I
Impulse control . . . .

K
Kitchen dresser . . . .

L
Life skills . . . .

M
Microchip . . . .
Motivation . . . .
Multiple-cat household . . . .

N
Nail trimming . . . .
Nose target . . . .

O
Overweight . . . .

P
Paw target . . . .
Phase, sensitive . . . .
Place of retreat . . . .
Prohibitions . . . .
Puberty . . . .
Punishment . . . .

R
Reward . . . .
Ritual . . . .
Roughness . . . .

S
Scratching tree . . . .
Scratching / marking . . . .
Scratching points . . . .
Self-control, psychomotoric . . . .
Security . . . .
Selection . . . .
Sit target . . . .

Socialisation . . . .
Starting box game. . . . .

T
Target exercises . . . .
Thundershirt®. . . . .
Tolerance . . . .
Toothbrushing. . . . .
Transport bag . . . .
Transport box . . . .

V
Valerian. . . . .
Visits to the vet . . . .

W
Walks . . . .
Want of hygiene . . . .
Wish box. . . . .
Whole-body wrap . . . .
Working meal . . . .